Tradition and Change
A Study of 20th Centruy Indian Thought

TRADITION AND CHANGE

(A Study of 20th Century Indian Thought)

Gopinath N Sharma

1994

KAVERI BOOKS

DELHI-110085

ISBN 81-7479-002-0

Published by : Rakesh Goel
Kaveri Books
125, Kadambari, 19/IX, Rohini,
Delhi-110085 (India)
Ph. 7265687

Laser Typeset by : Delite Printers, Delhi

Printed at : Raj Offset Works, Delhi

PRINTED IN INDIA

For Peggy

It is a wonder how you
alone are not tired of me!
— Gopi

Acknowledgements

I am highly indebted to Dr. H.A. Gani, Reader, Department of Political Science, Marathwada University, Aurangabad, for his guidance and encouragement. He has always been keen on helping me during the preparation of this work. But for his efforts I should have found it impossible to arrive at this stage.

It is very sad that Prof. Dr. Moin Shakir, former Head, Department of Political Science, Marathwada University, Aurangabad, under whom I had just begun working for this topic, did not live to see the completion of this project.

I wish to take this opportunity to thank Shri Rakesh Goel, Publisher, Kaveri Books for having released this book in such a short duration. Nothing can run parallel to my sister-in-law, Dr. (Mrs.) Chitra Sharma's and Dr. B. P. Engade's consistent encouragement. In fact, they do not know how much they have tolerated me.

Gopinath N Sharma

Acknowledgements

I am highly indebted to Dr. H.A. Gadkari, the Department of Political Science, Marathwada University, for his guidance and encouragement. He has always been helping me during the preparation of this work; without his efforts I should have found it impossible to complete...

It is very sad that Prof. Dr. Mohan Singh, Department of Political Science, Marathwada University, passed under whom I had can begun working for this... see the completion of this project.

I wish to take this opportunity to thank my... publisher, Kaveri Books, for having published this work in short duration. Nothing can run parallel to... Dr. (Mrs.) Chitra Sharma's and Dr. B. R. Engade... encouragement. In fact they do not know how much they tolerated me.

Gopinath...

Contents

1

Introduction

Over the ages, unity of India has been symbolized by a cultural continuity, embodied into a unified principle of consciousness,[1] which has contributed to the identity of its 'inner-structure'.[2] This inner structure primarily lies in the religious principles and their interpretations.[3] There is no doubt that tradition and modernity are quite contrary to each other. In order to understand clearly the interaction between them, and how far modernity can really prevail, it is necessary to know what the term 'tradition' implies. Tradition consists of historically shaped customs, rites, social precepts, ideas, values, rules of conduct etc. It is handed down from generation to generation.[4] Tradition has also been defined as "the aggregate of customs, beliefs, and practices, that give continuity to a culture, civilization or social group and thus shape its views; taken in this sense, laws and institutions are also part of tradition."[5] Moreover, tradition can be progressive, if it is meant to deal with a culture. This is because no culture can afford to remain static and therefore, it undergoes changes to fulfil the demands and meet the challenges, of the new age.

Nevertheless, it must be borne in mind that the authoritative tone of tradition brings the scope of its further development to a standstill. According to Milton Singer: "Culture change, like any other kind of change, has a temporal dimension which is useful to distinguish into linear and cyclical varieties. Linear type of culture changes imply a specification of a date or approximate date which allows us to fix a 'before' and 'after' division. Modernization of a cultural tradition is a linear type of change in this sense. It implies that tradition has been transformed which it did not have before a certain date ... Not all changes which the tradition undergoes in the modern period, however, result into modernization... It is useful, in other words, to consider whether the result of any particular change in tradition is continuous with the structure prevailing before a certain date, or whether that structure has been replaced by a new change. In the former case we might speak of the change as a traditionalizing type, in the latter as a modernizing type... If the change results in a structure which is neither quite like the traditional one nor a predominantly new one, we might speak of a compromise formation."[6]

It has been observed that traditions left to themselves are transient in nature and highly susceptible to change, provided they do not merge into history and become contribution to historical development. This is perhaps one of the main reasons as to why we have classified traditions into little traditions and great traditions. This is an indication that modernity is truly concerned with the reformation of traditions but not as usually conceived, involved in the elimination of traditions. There have been many factors influencing the dynamicism of traditions and are mostly external factors. One such factor that demands our attention is cultural renaissance. This, in addition to the reformations, has to a large extent a bearing on the great traditions. Their wider scope points towards textual and contexual significances. However, in case of little traditions, it is the contextual significance that causes a cultural change. Thus, both little and great traditions lead to a cultural mobility and social change. Sanskritisation may be regarded as little tradition while those traditions emerging out of rejection of the fundamental principles of hierarchy are considered as great traditions. However, such a classification depends upon the manner in which a concept is evaluated within the scale of textual or contextual norms. At times it is very difficult to identify the pattern of a tradition as it covers large area. Although it has to display simple facts, it deals with the complex design of the society. Nevertheless, its own texture appears to be unintelligible. As Louis Dumont says: "The difficulty is that the thing is true at the same time at a multitude of levels. Each field of thought, each point of view itself rests upon a simplification, but thought it discursive and it cannot only explore one field, but make on point of view succeed another and by combining in this way different simplifications, reconstruct the complexity of the datum... If common thought simplifies itself in this way at each instant, the vocation of the sociologist is, in this sense, inverse. His understanding consists in replacing the simple in the complex, the small in the great, in lighting up a restricted area by bringing back to its environment, which common thought (and often following it, thought in general) suppresses. The sociologist has to construct a view in which the representation is preserved as it presents itself and at the same time is seen in its relation to its non-conscious counterpart."[7] Thus, traditions little as well as great, very often seem to be effective for a limited time and only few of them revive.

Sources of Indian Tradition

There is no denying the fact that various religious and philosophies play an important role in shaping the traditions and thereby enriching the culture heritage. As far as India is concerned the cultural traditions owe a good deal for their origin to the dominant religion, i.e., Hinduism and philosophy. Nonetheless, this cannot be considered as a unique feature since the cultural heritage of any country with its vast history certainly indicates its temperament through religion and philosophy. Despite this, it is pertinent to note that in West and East alike, only those religions which have earned recognition at the universal level and continue to remain as a source of the country's or region's traditions are given importance. As it is remarked : "Between the fifth century B.C. and the fourth century A.D., India brought into flower the great devotional religion of Hinduism. It is unlike any Western faith. It has Gods that number in the millions, any of whom - from all to none — may be adored with equal propriety. It has not a fixed system of worship; some Hindus pray, others meditate, others make sacrifices. It has no single prophet, who codified and evangelized its beliefs, rather it developed from the primitive worship of the forces of nature and the Vedic philosophy of India's dim past. And yet underlying this strange assemblage of ideas and holy figures, combined and transmuted from several beginnings, is a solid foundation of commonly held belief to unify the diversity that is India."[8]

One of the peculiar characteristics of the Indian philosophy or tradition is that it tries to accommodate different schools of thought especially those with heterogeneous character and seeks a balance through them. History reveals that the sources of Indian philosophical traditions are set of religious beliefs which are found in the Vedas and Vedanta. The first development of the philosophical views gave rise to sharp conflicts. This was also the reason for the erection of systems. In order to gain supremacy over the contemporary and rival systems, every system attempted to reinforce its original ideas in a different manner. The propounders adopted almost identical techniques to go through the discipline of Purvapaksha (exposing rival standpoint or view or claim) and Siddhanta (explaining in detail the inference drawn).

Brahminism, though does not account for the spirit of the most ancient religion of the Indian subcontinent, yet stands as a system of belief and rituals, Indians have always considered it as the source of their religious traditions. Later on Hinduism did hang onto it, while Buddhism could dare to reject much of it. Even today, the former to some extent sticks to the formal literature, the Veda, which has survived for ages together. Another most significant source of religious ideas, came from the Aryans who invaded India from the North-European traditions—particularly those of Iran, Greece and Rome. One of the most important features of this period had been the emergence of an 'idea' which insisted for the sacrifice of human beings. Thus, for the first time in history the orthodox schools of thought regarded humanity above divinity and urged upon the ethical values. As it is said: "When Aryans finally established the supremacy of their faith, all other objects of worship became subsidiary to their High God Brahman. This developing monotheism, however, was imperfect; other Gods still held varying power and influence over the people. Nevertheless, during this Vedic period (1200-500 B.C.) a unitive theme in their religion was developing. The Rig Veda is a collection of metrical hymns to Gods as nature powers and these hymns contain clear signs of perceiving God in an impersonal way. In the hymn to the Unknown God,......it is indicated that God cannot be described or treated like a person even though he exists. Like many ancient peoples the Aryans believed that the creation of the universe and of human beings resulted from the sacrifice of a cosmic being. The "idea" of sacrifice to the Aryans was more important than the Gods themselves. These sacrifices (Yajana) and the mysterious powers they evoked (Dharma) implied a great impersonal force at work in the universe."[9] The rigid classification of the schools into the orthodox and the heterodox brought into light the Vedic and anti-Vedic attitudes and the traditions. The former includes Purva-Mimamsa (Veda), Uttara Mimansa (Vedanta), Sankhya, Yoga, Nyaya and Vaisesika, while the latter comprises Lokayata, Buddhism and Jainism.

In the last century Hindu religious thought underwent a drastic change due to certain factors. This had its immediate influence over the traditions in vogue. This period may be regarded as a period of transvaluation of the existing social structure, religions, customs, traditions etc. It gave rise to various socio-religious movements namely, the Brahmo Samaj (the society of God). The Prarthana Samaj (the Brahmo idea in Maharashtra), the Arya Samaj (outcome of the principle of Revivalism), The Ramkrishna Movement and also the Theosophical Movement. Of all these, Theosophical movement deserves our attention because at that time a large number of Europeans rejected Western civilization and became rather rabid partisans of Indian culture. It was in 1875, that Madame Blavatsky and Colonel Olcott founded the Theosophical society, which held in great reverence the reincarnations and Karma theory along with Hindu and Buddhist conceptions as central doctrines. As it is pointed out: "European influences—whether friendly or hostile - of necessity played but a secondary role in the renascence of Hinduism. It was primarily through the efforts of a series of devout and devoted men that this ancient religion was able to recover in such a remarkable manner the deepest sources of its original inspiration."[10]

Therefore, the Western secular institutions and missionary activities despite exerting great pressure on Hindu society failed to prevent the emergence of a Hindu stand in the second half of the nineteenth century. At the same time, classical Indian thought attracted many of the European scholars, who gave momentum to the Hindu revival. Similarly, a large number of creative individuals from the ranks of Hindu society came forward to respond to the combined challenge of the pervading Christian religious ideas, modern Western rationalism and, to some extent, the utilitarian thought. Thus, Hinduism found favourable atmosphere to improve its position, despite the facts that law and order remained under British administration during that period.

The Course of Indian Philosophical Tradition

It is important to note that Indian philosophy is considered to be an offshoot of religion. However, the word philosophy and religion do not convey the same meaning. Therefore, it would be wrong to dub Indian philosophy as only religious philosophy and nothing else. This is due to the fact that the ideas, doctrines and theories of Indian philosophy are not consistent with any particular mode of presentation nor do they seem to have grown out of any religion. The different systems which developed are either spiritual or materialistic, theistic or atheistic. The two words commonly used by the ancient and classical thinkers of India had been *darsana* and *mata*, which are significant even today. They mean seeing or viewing of an opinion or thought respectively.

No doubt, religion comprises dogmas, which ought to be unquestionably accepted and followed. However, we find a good deal of difference in their interpretation as far as India is concerned. This is obvious from the fact that Mimamsa interpretation calls for strong faith in the Vedic scriptures, while Jainism, Buddhism reject the same. Similarly, Nyaya, the Yoga and some of the Vedantic schools accept a personal God, while the early Mimamsa, the Sankhya, Jainism, Buddhism reject the same. They do not accept any dogmatic authority but believe in experience and reason. Despite this, all these schools are treated as religious and the sources of spiritual philosophies of India. Since from the beginning the Indian traditions known as 'Sampradayas', were highly reflective and it is not surprising that in due course of time they became philosophies. It should be noted that the philosophical traditions in India do not differ from one another on every point. In fact, their ethical and social grounds have much in common and they follow the Mimamsa school. However, on metaphysical grounds they had certain differences. Some of them were pluralistic and realistic while others were idealistic and absolutist. This was the reason that they could influence each other in some way or the other.

Needless to say that the major problems of philosophy in ancient period centred round the nature of the Universe, man's place in the Universe, ethical codes, scope of free-will, fate, immortality, mind and matter etc. Even today, more or less the same problems have engaged the minds of the philosophers and as such they attempt to find out some solutions for them. With the advancement in science however phenomenalism came to prominence by rejecting "the notion that there are forever inaccessible objects shrouded behind the veil of appearance by reducing all talk of things perceived or perceivable to talk about actual or possible perceptual experience.[11] However, metaphysical problems remained unresolved and they continue to raise their heads. Even modernity has to a large extent failed to, succeed in this regard.

A cursory glance at the Indian philosophy shows that spiritual interests have always dominated in Indian society,[12] and as such persistent attempts had been made to save it from empirical attitudes. In the recent past, this tendency assumed the form of philosophical traditions in India. Despite this we are not quite sure about the factions which led to the emergence of so many divergent views at such an early period of our history. At best it can be said that Indian philosophy is highly complicated and lays great emphasis on defining and building up systems and thereby explores as much as possible in the past. This appears to most of the critics as a permanent nostalgic feeling which may prove to be quite damaging. Nevertheless, it is pointed out: "All these, surprisingly enough, have peacefully coexisted with the most remarkable logical subtleties and dialectical abilities, a peculiarity really difficult to understand for one acquainted only with the European tradition."[13]

On account of this, the materialists hold the view that unlike the European philosophy, there is nothing in the Indian philosophy which could strike at the traditional beliefs and fancies. Besides, as the beliefs have close bearing on sentiments it becomes difficult to eliminate them at any stage. However, the materialists or Lokayatas remained by far as the only exception to this. Their basic view was to rely on the primacy of sense perception as the source of valid knowledge and straightway reject the authority drawn from scriptures. A large number of Indian philosophers were not very much enthusiastic to examine the ancestral beliefs in the light of the developing knowledge. However, this was not because the ancient beliefs did not permit any intellectual development.

Considering the views of those who found all marvel only in the Indian philosophy, one feels that Indian philosophers even after attaining philosophical heights, somehow were eager to hold a tolerant corner in their minds to the traditions, which in fact needed a renewal. It may be said that there existed a typical relationship between the primitive beliefs and the new or advanced philosophical heights. In the words of Max Muller, "India has always been — a world of thinkers, a nation of philosophers". It was at any rate impossible to ignore the proven scientific facts, as well as the deductions drawn thereof. It is under this state of continuing conflict that Indian philosophy marched through a couple of centuries. This resulting state of conflicts could not escape the attention of the thinkers from East as well as West. Thus the ever growing entropean world produced a hazy picture in patches. Therefore, Indian philosophy faces numerous challenges even today as in the past.

Nevertheless, Indian philosophy is unique and its importance cannot be undermined. As S. Radhakrishnan and Charles Moore pointed out: "The study of Indian philosophy is important historically, philosophically, and even politically. The Indian philosophical tradition is man's oldest as well as the longest continuous development of speculation about the nature of reality and man's place therein. It began with the ancient Vedas, which are probably the earliest documents of the human mind that have come down to us, and has continued age after age in progressive philosophical advance in the effort to understand life and reality. But it is not as a piece of antiquarian investigation that we of today should study Indian philosophy. Despite the tendency to respect and revere the greatness of the past, Indian thinkers of all ages have been deeply and profoundly concerned with the ultimate truth which is timeless. Nor should we study Indian philosophy as a merely provincial or geographical approach to reality. Despite changes by some western critics who would accuse Indian philosophy of neglecting scientific method, Indian thinkers have not been anti-empirical and have not neglected nature in their study of reality; nor, in their study of man, have they been excessively restricted to those characteristics which may be peculiar to man in India. India's concentrated study of the inner nature of man is, in the end, a study of man universal."[14]

Thus, it is obvious that despite a great deal of western influence and the development of science, the philosophical traditions in India remained intact due to their link with the religious-philosophical trends. Had the Indian traditions been purely philosophical and destitute of the religious overtone and the mythological ingredients, perhaps the picture would have been quite different.

Philosophical Traditions

As far as the Indian philosophical traditions are concerned

there had been different opinions, and some of them are quite damageable. No doubt, the various systems of Indian philosophy and certain sects look to the ancient scriptures as absolutely infallible sources, yet, it has been commented that they are guesses at truth and are not systematic philosophy.[15] It is quite true that even in Vedas the centre of interest was the outward fact. Therefore, Reality was sought in the objective universe. This shows that Indian philosophical systems did not just concentrate on the metaphysics but also on Naturalism. Thus they did not have frail resources, as usually thought.

The philosophical traditions are offshoots of our own problems and inquiry. The difference between traditions and the traditionalism is well-illustrated by the following statements: "The difference between the traditions of the traditionalists and philosophical traditions lies in the latter being avowedly self-respective. Otherwise even thorough going logicalism will have to be called a type of traditionalism. Many thought-forms and their impulses are rooted in our life and aim at throwing light on the different aspects of life. Sometimes they overlap and become confused. To remove the confusions, thought generates forms of self-reflection and creates traditions of methodology, epistemology, and logic like the Nyaya in India. These methodological traditions overlap other traditions and create new problems; then philosophical thought may be pushed further and further from its origins."[16] Hence, according to Indian thinkers traditions emerge when the various currents of philosophical thought maintain contact with their origin and continue to express the same spirit.

Since classical philosophies in India have continued to be the philosophies of life they can be easily categorised. They constitute different traditions on the basis of human nature and philosophical perspectives. Most of the philosophical traditions in India came into being in ancient time and later on due to the deviations. The principle of action which implies a pluralistic universe was widely acceptable preposition. The nature of pluralistic universe cannot be explained without reference to the theory of action. Therefore, it became the supreme principle. The tradition of action or its metaphysical implications are called Mimamsa tradition. In order to understand and evaluate, the forms and methods of these implications, referring to other traditions, such as, the Nyaya and the Vaisesika becomes essential. We also have the Sankhya and the Yoga traditions. Lastly, a tradition is needed to explain the bond of self and the surrounding world. In this regard, the Vedanta tradition played the pivotal role. Thus, it is obvious that unlike traditions in the west, the philosophical traditions in India, cannot be represented in a sequence. The traditions emerge in response to man's need. Right from the period of early Aryans, attempts have been made to overcome nature and the first two parts of Veda on which the Mimamsa philosophy is based can be cited to substantiate this. As far as Mimamsa philosophy is concerned, it was truly an orthodox tradition. Later on the Carvaka, Jainism and Buddhism came into being as reactions to Mimamsa. Nyaya, Vaisesika and Yoga accepted the scriptural authority of Veda to some extent. Vedanta seems to have aligned itself with the spirit of the latter parts of the Veda. No doubt, there is difference of opinion as far as the order of the traditions is concerned. Nevertheless, there is no denying the fact that they are the sources of philosophical traditions.

Nature of Indian Philosophy

There is no doubt that every philosophy to a certain extent bears the mark of its 'origin'. Therefore, despite the alterations in its attitudes the spirit remains intact. To substantiate this argument various examples can be cited here. The British philosophy sounds highly empirical; American philosophy with William James's, 'Pragmatism' seems to be leaning towards realistic considerations and to quote James' phrase, 'towards cash value'. Similarly, according to Cartesian theory, French philosophy lends support to absolutely rationalistic outlook; which has the scientific temperament. On the other hand, German philosophy, as described in Kant's critique of pure reason, practical reason and judgement, Hegel's idealism and Schopenhauer's pessimism, had to go through rigorous idealism or a speculative workshop. In view of this, it is difficult to point out the nature of Indian philosophy or compare it with any particular 'ism'. Nevertheless, it can be said that the Indian philosophy does not restrict itself to any specific behavioural doctrine as from the time immemorial it continues to be meditative. Since the meditative process has to always deal with varieties of human temperament and practically sail over than smothering them it is difficult to determine the form of Indian philosophy. Radhakrishnan says: "Indian philosophy has its interests in the haunts of men and not in supra lunar solitudes. It takes its origin in life and enters back into life after passing through the schools—the Gita and the Upanishads are not remote from popular belief. They are the great literature of the country and at the same time vehicles of the great systems of thought. The Puranas contain the truth dressed up in myths and stories to suit the weak understanding of the majority. The hard task of interesting multitude in metaphysics is achieved in India."[17]

Thus, it can be said that the Indian philosophy or ancient Hindu thoughts being indifferent to history failed to provide link with the thoughts of the modern philosophers. The ancient and mediaeval Indian writers seem to be very much concerned about the authenticity of doctrines or ideals. As Sir Charles Eliot says, "The truly religious mind does not care for the history of religion, just as among us, the scientific mind does not dwell on the history of science."[18] On the other hand, the Western writers at present make much use of history, however, they too failed to accomplish what they aimed at.

Thus a rigidity remained for long, caused by the adherence to the past. Fortunately, there was also the growth of a multifarious philosophical pattern. This is however, not endorsed by the writers who support only Hindu thought. A number of alternate standpoints also could have emerged; on dint of which though contradictions were necessary, but would have provided an isolated system. However, the law of dialectics could not come forth and therefore, though clash and conflict remained, yet nothing emerged in the mediaeval period out of the fundamental differences. Later on, there were difficulties in the rebuilding of the original spirit. There were subjective idealists who took delight in the thought and its self-creating and all producing powers. There were those who refused to identify reality in terms of thought and matter. Of late the traditional scholars began explaining everything new which they discovered and felt that these have true potentiallty but they could do so in the old form of thoughts. In the light of this they were forced to contradict the earlier presumptions and that is why they developed a radical difference.

If the age old historical account of Indian philosophy and the loyalty of its followers are considered, then one can understand that it is indeed difficult to rupture at once the bond of traditions and make a beginning afresh. Another encouraging fact for them had been the accommodative nature of Indian philosophy. Owing to this it has developed a tendency to provide sufficient scope to explore the established as well as upcoming isms. Therefore, it is exceedingly difficult to decide the nature of Indian philosophy, nevertheless, many have hastened to make it spiritual.

The roots of Indian philosophy can be traced back in the field of Rg 'Veda. Incidentally, the speculative activities remained uninterrupted, despite foreign influence on them. This kind of experiment is discernible and can be studied through the authoritative system evolved of that time. They constitute the structure of Indian philosophy. The period can also be looked upon as a unique one, for the emergence of Brahminism, restricted to nation and Buddhism with an allowance to enjoy the status of a world religion. At this stage, it appears that even philosophical theory of the universe has to face the ethical consequences, until it gets stabilised. Therefore, eternal philosophical truths rarely appear decisive or something like a striking expression. As it is said: "The function of history, as we conceive it, is therefore, to examine the content of life. We have seen that life is not atomistic, in spite of appearances, but that is purposive; that is not a mere drift, but a striving. There is a definite tendency underlying existence—a tendency to reach to perfection. Thus human endeavour is not ruled by mere conflict and diversity; there is a principle of unity which reveals a world or Reason. It is only a partial and sectional view that presents contradictions and inconsistencies.[19] Thus, it can be said that going through the dialectics may not help to form a perfect philosophy or attitude.

It is interesting to note that the Indian philosophy having every shade of speculation does not lead to pessimism. Therefore, it would be unreasonable to say that it represents total negation or indirectly suggests—rather encourages inaction in toto, under the guise of detachment. The fact remains that the Indian philosophy while passing through such phases experienced a queer mixture of human temperament. Of course, since Indian philosophy has different tendencies, therefore, the criticism made by the West cannot be completely ignored. As it is remarked: "While for example the prevailing spirit of the songs included in the Rg Veda is optimistic, there is sometimes a note of sadness in them as in those addressed to the goddess of Dawn which pointedly refer to the way in which she cuts short the little lives of men."[20]

Thus, a flow of intimately blending currents produces a mixed note of reactions which are difficult to analyse. In facts, this flow has been spread over a fairly long period and as such the scholars feel that the nature of Indian philosophy is influenced with both optimism and pessimism. According to S. Radhakrishnan: " We should delve with reverence into the pregnant archives of our past, if we wish to seek to know the ground we stand on the road we travel, and the reason why."[21]

Unfortunately, the past is often presented in our everyday experience as a reactionary force, concentrated in the yoke of custom and manifested in meaningless ceremonials, which are a mere drag on our free initiative.[22] Due to this we are compelled to think that the alterations in the traditions of past are essential for the progress. This may at times even lead to conflict between tradition and environment.

East and West

It must be borne in mind that although the Eastern and Western philosophers, thinkers or writers pursue the same goals, their approaches widely differ. In view of this, it is necessary to draw a line of demarcation between them. Eastern attitudes remained indifferent to the historical and chronological details. Of course, this does not apply to the modern period. On the other hand, from the beginning, the western philosophers were meticulous to maintain an orderliness and present everything in a systematic manner. According to D.S. Sarma, "One of the characteristics of ancient Hindu thought is its indifference to history. In discussing the contents of a book for instance, ancient and even mediaeval Indian writers care very little for the date or life of the author. They care more for the truth of experience or soundness of doctrine than for circumstances that gave it birth."[23]

It becomes clear that from the very beginning, the Indian philosophers followed a style related to the theory of formalism, in order to extend with all possible means, the contents of the subject. Probably this could be regarded the 'Essence' that mattered most to the eastern philosophers and, therefore, they remained indifferent to the form of presentation. This neither caused any serious difficulty nor lowered the status of Indian philosophers. Moreover, their sincerity was also not suspected. However, it is important that due to lack of continuity, they have been subjected to unjust criticism. Although it is not difficult to find out the exact historical point at which the Indian philosophy or philosophical traditions came into contact with the western counterpart, it seems traditions in India were already burdened by religious sentiments and loyalty thereof. On the other hand Western tradition had just emerged victorious with its achievements through Industrial Revolution. This had been one of the reasons as to why western tradition was "steeped in philosophies of optimism, of universal progress, rationalism and hedonism."[24]

In view of this, modern writers whether they belong to East or West concentrate on historical facts and make every possible effort to find out the roots.

Another important point which differentiates them is that many a time, priority of moral value or rationality to other types of value has been questioned. The idealists were inclined to treat scientific value as subsidiary to virtue. The philosophers like Nietsche and Eckhart in the past questioned the supremacy of moral values on the grounds that there were other values. There was a general tendency to defend a few and ignore those who had genuine desire to contribute to the humanity. As Potter has described: "We weep for Socrates, defender of reason, damned by the citizens of Athens on the trumped-up charge of corrupting the youth but do not bother to investigate Nietzsche damned without examination by the citizens of the modern world on the trumped-up charge of being responsible for Hitler."[25]

Hence, in order to understand the thoughts of either East or West, it is essential to determine the ultimate values of a culture. It is necessary to consider what is of paramount importance in the lives of the people of that culture. This could be done by referring to the ideals of its wisest men. By and large, it appears that throughout the history of tradition of either, there has been consistently a sort of commitment to certain notions. These notions were developed in pursuit of certain goals. There was no clash regarding the attempts made by the followers of different cultures as they were exclusively the concepts aimed at, to suit the temperament of its people. Later on, when these concepts assumed a supreme ethical form, they were put to the usual test of moral perfection. Similarly, speculative philosophy was dominated by the intrinsic leaning towards freedom and as such a release from bondage was the primary concern. Having examined Eastern and Western approaches, it can be said that there is no question of any divorce in this regard. Although they have different forms of speculation, however, their efforts are directed towards similar understanding of self and control. What is needed is the art of introducing the principles underlying a culture or the stages of it that have led to the constitution of philosophy. As it is pointed out: "In introducing Indian philosophy to Western audiences it has been fashionable either to avoid all discussion of ultimate values or else to gloss over the fact unpalatable to the mainstream of Western thinkers that Indian philosophy does in fact elevate power, control or freedom to a superеminent position, above rational morality, shrouding this difference in a mist of vague platitudes above the unity of all religions and peoples and the moral preferability of seeing Indian and Western thought as one, whether they really agree or not. Indian philosophers have themselves been responsible for this latter fashion but it is important to note that they have not been Indians trained in traditional Hindu ways and governed accordingly, but rather westernized Indians, speaking and writing in Western languages, who wish to be heard in the Western community of scholars and to be accepted among them. The traditional Indian scholars have infrequently been heard on this point, a result not only of the language barrier but also of their lack of interest, in keeping with their heritage, in proselytizing or in seeking favour as if that were of importance in itself."[26]

It seems that Indian philosophy was prone to different shades of moral and ethical parameters which caused great difficulties for the scholars. Even at present it deals with the different problems of metaphysics, ethics, epistemology, psychology, logic etc. Each problem is considered by the Indian philosophers from all possible angles which is called a synthetic outlook.

It is necessary to note that although various scholars have different opinions regarding Indian philosophy, however, everyone acknowledges its spirit. According to Charles A. Moore: "The principles, attitudes and methods which are by rather common agreement, considered characteristics of Indian philosophy as a whole."[27] M. Hiriyanna points out: " One of its refusals to make a sharp distinction between philosophy and religion is characteristic; religion and philosophy do not stand sundered in India, the reason being that their purpose is in the last resort the same, a seeking for the central meaning of human existence."[28] Jadunath Sinha writes: "Philosophy and Religion have common objects. Both of them try to grasp the nature of the Universe and to understand man's place, function, and destiny in it."[29] For S.V.Venkateshwara: "Indian philosophy is not the denial but fulfilment of religion."[30] Similarly, Dhirendra M. Datta says: "Its attempts to base philosophy on all aspects of experience and not simply on sense experience deserves special attention as does its conviction that the ultimate reality manifests itself, or can be conceived in different ways."[31] S. Radhakrishnan opines: "If we can abstract from the variety of opinion and observe the general spirit of Indian thought, we shall find, it has a disposition to interpret life and nature in the way of monastic disposition."[32] Likewise P.T. Raju writes: "In Western philosophy one school or system generally develops out of another, and each philosopher brands his thought with a new name. In India, on the contrary, every philosopher considers it an honour to belong to one or the other school, whatever differences he may have from his predecessors in the same school, and considers himself as an intepreter and elaborator of his teacher's thoughts. Even when the differences are very marked, he would still treat himself as belonging to that tradition of thought."[33].

A glance at the course of Western philosophy shows that efforts had always been made to dominate contemporary currents. The traditional clash between metaphysical and materialistic attitude well illustrates this. The philosophers, such as, Thomas Aquinas of 13th century, George Berkeley of 18th century and Soren Kierkegaard of 19th century, had their own methods to judge, or even assert, 'truths' as described by religions. They tried to eliminate the errors in religions caused by materialistic as well as rationalistic outlooks. According to them, these errors were responsible for the steady decline of philosophy.

Similarly, Pythagoras, Rene' Descavtes and Bertrand Russell are basically mathematicians. Nevertheless, their views which centred around the theory of numbers led them to find out a new concept for understanding the universe and its phenomena. The other category of philosophers like Plato, Thomas Hobbes and J.S. Mill were very much concerned with the problems of political science and sociology. Apart from these two subjects they contributed in the allied areas. Their main motto was to deal with the behavioural sciences of men.

Likewise, we are also familiar with Milesians, Francis Bacon and in the present century, Alfred North Whitehead an exclusive group of philosophers—who concentrated on the physical plane of the natural world.[34] Thus, it becomes clear that by and large, the Western philosophers in order to understand the physical world wanted to know its intricate composition. They preferred to concentrate on metaphysics as a necessary process in philosophy's progress. Positivism can be cited here as an example of a definite type of philosophic tradition which strictly dealt with the religious convictions in the West. The positivists proposed a scientific method for enunciating clarity in philosophical assumptions and owing to this all philosophical tenets originating from religion had to undergo a rational verification as prescribed by science. Indeed this was a major breakthrough for West. As far as East is concerned, philosophers presented theories, which could not be verified. For example, belief in truths 'fall outside the method of 'verification'. Though this sounds metaphysically correct, yet on the empirical grounds, it is very difficult to accept the very concept. Probably owing to this philosophy in the East had to suffer a great deal. Moreover, it is held that the philosophy in the East emphasised its weakness in order to obtain the support of the religious values. Thus, its attachment to religion and indifference to science caused an irreparable loss. All these pave way for uncertainity and indirectly for setting aside the loud claims of the philosophical systems in vogue. However, Indian philosophical traditions were not very much keen to demarcate a distinct line, separating an area for understanding own freedom and the world of reality. In short, with all its various deficiencies, it allows its speculative philosophical pattern coupled with the problem of freedom only.

It is worth noting although positivism began in the west with a strong appeal and had developed absolute rational thinking on the basis of science, yet it was not free from contradictions. Even John S. Mill who earnestly attempted to achieve accurate and applied knowledge failed to realise the fatal narrowness of his concept which was restricted to a definite and rigid, system of values. As far as Russell is concerned, it can be said that he was quite confident of discovering strict logical rules for solving the philosophical problems of his time. In this way, various attempts were made to resolve the growing contradictions inherited from the earlier form of positivism. It is said: "In positivism, like in many other philosophical schools, one should always distinguish between the ideas of the classics and their followers. The former representing progressive tendencies in science, can usually be identified, first and foremost, by their profound devotion to the Goddess of philosophy and, alas, by sometimes no less profound delusions. Unlike the wholehearted founders of positivism, their numerous mediocre imitators lack the necessary critical spirit of trailblazers in science and, instead of exploiting the success of their forerunners and rising to a higher level, fall to aggravating their shortcomings and debasing their fruitful ideas."[35]

In facts, Bertrand Russell, Rudolf Carnap, Ludwing Wittgenstein and a few others deserve appreciation for having struggled to bring science and philosophy close even at the cost of their self-disparagement. The rapid development of experimental science in the 18th and 19th centuries, gave rise to the illusion that all problems of natural and social development could be solved exclusively by empirical means. It was also considered that the same techniques could be used in all fields. Moreover, the metaphysics in Indian philosophy is supposed to be always going hand in hand with religious thinking. No doubt, religion has played an outstanding role in shaping philosophical presumptions yet this cannot be treated as unique since in other countries it has proved to be effective with varying degrees. Comte, the positivist, rejects metaphysics; wherein he considers anything that crosses the limits of science - religion, idealism, materialism, dialectics - but again thinks that metaphysics is not entirely identical with religious thinking. To him, it prepares mankind for a transition to scientific thinking. A metaphysical thought is, so to speak, an intermediary between the theological and the scientific ways of thinking and performs simultaneously a critical function in relation to science.[36]

Western Criticism

Needless to say that the nature of Indian philosophy due to its religious overtones and its remaining more or less religious became a matter of great discussion among the western intellectuals and they even suspected its contribution to the academic philosophy. No doubt, it is quite true that in India, religion and philosophy go hand in hand and it is difficult to fix their boundaries. This is mainly because they have more or less common goals. For example, both of them aim at seeking the real cause of human existence. This does not mean that the Western philosophers have not made any attempt to solve the riddle of human existence through religion and philosophy. However, these two approaches are considered different because of the difference in their modes. In India too, this kind of difference is discernable, nevertheless, it is never looked upon as divorce.[37] Therefore, it can be said that the Indian philosophy to certain extent resembles that in the West. According to Mrs. Rhys Davids, Science, Philosophy and Religion are 'an armed truce' in West.[38]

In the West, the conscious mind is used to explore the external world, whereas it is expected to be used to explore the internal world. This is because the development of psychology made the Western mind conscious of the necessity of gaining knowledge of the internal world. In fact, from the ancient time, there have been outstanding exceptions to mystical philosophers. Both Eastern and Western systems believe that the mind is the arbiter of reality and, therefore, a good deal of attention has been focused on it to reveal the secrets of mind. The philosophers of the East and the West do not hold the same view about the concept of mind. The Easterners consider mind as the true vehicle for transcendence, while the westerns opine that it consists of instincts, ego, weakness and illness etc. This difference is mainly because most of the modern psychologists reject the idea of mind as being anything more than an epiphenomenon of the brain. This has led V. Brodov to remark: "It has become a kind of tradition with some British and American scholars to clothe Indian philosophical thought in mysticism, considering it mostly in its religious aspects and even identifying it with religious thought. The theoretical sources of this tradition are quite old. It was Hegel who wrote, "What we refer to as Eastern philosophy is, generally speaking, to a much greater extent a religious mode of perception and a religious world view of the Oriental peoples which can easily be mistaken for philosophy. The American philosopher William T. Harris (1835-1909) in his numerous works characterises Indian philosophy as negative absolutism, abstractionism and nihilism. This view has proved to be extremely tenacious and still has some adherents."[39] The Western philosophers believe that unlike in the west, the Indian philosophy lacks the systematic inquiry of things. As Thilly asserts: "Few of the ancient peoples advanced far beyond the mythological stage and perhaps none of them can be said to have developed a genuine philosophy except Greeks. The spirit of independence and the love of truth which animates their thinkers have never been surpassed and rarely equalled."[40]

Thus, it is obvious that from the beginning the philosophies of some of the countries have been either looked down upon or underestimated. On account of this, the oriental theories despite adopting similar methods for solving the problems of philosophy got a rough deal at the hands of the westerners. One of their common complaints had been: "Even the theories of orient peoples, the Hindus, Egyptians and Chinese consist in the main, of mythological and ethical doctrines and are not complete systems of thoughts they are pervaded with poetry and faith.[41]

In fact, the traditional studies in the history of Indian philosophy have a scholarly value, and the translations of the original texts are available in a number of Indian and European languages. Moreover, the terminological difficulties and missing chronological dates, have been dealt with and the methodological discrepancies have been removed. However, the criticism levelled against the Indian philosophy does not hold water. Indian philosophy in the past was described as a singly whole though various schools did not see eye to eye on certain vital issues. Probably, the western critics failed to understand the concentric nature of the systems. Philosophy has been viewed as a manifestation or characteristic of an undaunted spirit of the whole Indian people. According to S. Radhakrishnan: "Philosophy in India is essentially spiritual. It is the intense spirituality of India, and not any great political structure or social organization that it has developed, that has enabled it to resist the ravages of time and the accidents of history..."[42]

A general comparison of western and Indian philosophers shows that the former confined their concentration to certain areas, while the latter were not indifferent even to the obscure aspects of the various sources of knowledge. Hence, western philosophers irrespective of any school of thought they belonged, consider the world and the life with ease. They argue: "Our existence may have its imperfections and shortcomings; but on that score it was not to be rejected; it has indeed, elements of value which cannot be ignored. Life, above all is a partnership; it is a great co-operative endeavour. It might be made richer and nobler by the sharing of experience. And it is manifestation of the Divine. Reality could be realised in and through it. The end of human life could be attained through love and service, under the conditions that make this our complex earthly existence..." On the other hand, the Indian philosophers consider the world to be miserable; and full of anxiety for those born here. Our earthly existence seems almost a blunder. The content of men's lives was abandoned as worthless and painful.

The spirit of India was in quest of immortality; sentient life, on the other hand, was a phantasmagoria, its delusion alone being real. The desire for the world is the desire for death; why, therefore, go after that through which the Eternal Soul cannot be gained! Thus speculation in India centred round the question, "What is Reality apart from the false world we see around us?"[43]

Therefore, it is apparent that the Western thought is quite optimistic in its approach whereas Indian thought is pessimistic. One of the main reasons for this is that like the schools of pessimism Indian philosophy does not whole-heartedly permit negative approach. The pessimism is quite obvious in its consideration of the ultimate phase of life. It appears that Indian philosophy is too much obsessed with the very concept of eternity and, therefore, it cannot easily digest the idea of death or that of spirit and consequently the idea of self. As far as the western optimism is concerned, it seems that the majority philosophers are happy by their methods of analysis at its face value. The western philosophy rejoices in the immediate results. Indian philosophers because of their application of elaborate methods fail to create enthusiam. Similarly, the western philosophers' anxiety and desperation for gaining quick rather than permanent solutions also create disappointment.

Even today in West a strong wave of prejudices continues and for various reasons Westerners have contempt for the Eastern schools. It is difficult to point out the main reason for this state of affairs, however, it can be said that the overall picture in both the West as well as East, is not a happy one. Dasgupta describes it as, "The achievements of the ancient Indians in the field of philosophy are but very imperfectly known to the world at large and it is unfortunate that the condition is no better even in India."[44]

Indian philosophy does not offer a corridor merely for metaphysical pursuits. Instead, it expects evolution of the righteous principles of life through 'experience'. The word 'Darsana' connotes the same meaning and as it can be easily cognized, lays a strong emphasis on individual's experience, feelings and judgements. Basically there is opposition to the very method of abstract reasoning. Probably this view must have provided an exclusive identity to Indian philosophy. Indian philosophy purveys a clue that realization for self from the transcendental state is valued more than a mere faith. In doing so, even if one forms an opinion that religion and philosophy are not separated, it cannot be overruled. However, there is as such no perpetual dependence either.[45]

Robert A. Hume justifies the Western attitudes towards Indian philosophy. He comments: "It has puzzled many a western student of Indian thought how and why there has been religion and philosophy. Generally speaking the preacher and the philosopher alike in the West deplore this alliance for quite opposite reasons. To the preacher it would appear that Hinduism is too philosophical to be a religion. He finds it a cold intellectualism, not an appeal to life, in all its aspects but an appeal to logic.[46]

In fact, Indian philosophy permits all the possible appropriation but does not consider any one attitude as leading one. It strongly recommends rearing up of a living philosophy provided it aims at concrete realization through routine experience. As Max Muller points out: "In India philosophy can be recommended not for the sake of knowledge but for the highest purpose that man can strive after his life."[47] Strangely enough, in spite of cultural differences and departure from each other's methodology, the basic philosophical problems and the solutions suggested by Indian and European traditions, are more or less the same. This kind of attitude appears to be on account of psychological bearing. The belief of the West that its method of philosophising is the right one, which yielded great results, led it to assume a superior, at times even a condenscending attitude vis-a-vis the Eastern thinkers. It seems to be so due to the appreciations of the holistic approach by the West while this is not the case with the east.

Indian Tradition and the Problem of Reality

It is important to note that as far as the problem of reality is concerned, East and West have a fundamental difference in their emphasis. The Western thought lays great stress on the analytical knowledge and believe that only this type of knowledge can properly guide them. As such in order to decide the nature of reality they advocate discarding of negative qualities and adhering to the positive ones. On the other hand, East believes in its innate tendency and acknowledges even contradictions as the possible facets of reality. This is because before arriving at some conclusion, it wants to study every problem from all possible perspectives. It goes to the extent of considering even error as a sort of partial truth.

Therefore, an attempt has been made to evaluate this aspect in order to indicate the value it carries.

Needless to say that in this regard the Indian viewpoint has been a moot point. Most of the thinkers opine that everything can be found in Vedas, which is the source of all secrets. Since these secrets are found in Vedas in the form of hymns, they need re-interpretation to convince the modern mind. This becomes more important as the modernity always demands brevity and conclusive remarks to suit it. On the other hand, the western philosophers opine that Indian philosophers have not made any sincere attempt to promote philosophical thought in order to enrich the academics of philosophy.

A.C. Underwood points out: "It is much to be regretted that no Indian philosopher is today doing creative work. Of living Indian philosophers, the one best known to the West is Prof. S. Radhakrishnan of Calcutta University. But in his published work he does not concern himself so much with the problems of contemporary philosophy as with the history of Hindu thought. Indeed he himself laments the lethargy which has overcome the philosophic impulse in India during the last three or four centuries and traces it to the Moslem invasion of India and to the propagandist work of Christian missions. In his opinion, both these factors have helped to inhibit the philosophical impulse of the Hindu mind and have driven it to seek shelter in the arms of convention and authority."[48]

It is a known fact that modernity and tradition do not get along well. Since modernity and tradition have developed a spirit of animosity, they can hardly be reconciled. Although, many a time modernity while attempting to solve problems tries to emulate the traditional thoughts. However, in this regard, it has not been very successful in overcoming the traditional barriers. Therefore, it can be said that modernity has no relevance without a reference to tradition. As it is observed: "Modernity has generally been opposed to tradition in contemporary analyses of social and political change. The roots of the opposition of modernity and tradition go back atleast as far as the enlightenment. Condorcet's unlinear vision of progress found nothing of value in the past and saw the hope of mankind in the future. His perspective is till to be found in the assumptions of those concerned to understand the course of modernization in new motions. So is Marx's variant of the enlightenment attitude. The idea of dialectical conflict denigrates the past in its assumptions that 'theses' will be consumed in the fires of revolutionary change. Building on such assumptions theorists of social change in new nations have found a dichotomy between tradition and modernity. Useless and valueless tradition has been relegated to a historical trash heap. Modernity will be realized when tradition has been destroyed, suspended. If tradition and modernity are seen as continuous, they are dialectically rather than dichotomously related and if internal variations are attended to and taken seriously, then those sectors of traditional society become critical for understanding."[49]

The survival of social, political or religious traditions depends upon their appraisal made by taking into consideration the changing circumstances. Today's modernity will evolve into tomorrow's tradition.

As far as the social changes in India are concerned, although several thinkers have expressed different opinions, however, everyone admits that religion, language-literature, and geographical conditions have dominated social changes. Moreover, there are a few other factors which contributed to this process, however, they are restricted to certain areas. Louis Dumont opines: "The study of social change in view of the nebulous nature of its theory is a difficult task and it is more difficult in the case of a society like India which has not only a fathomless historical depth and plurality of traditions but is also engulfed in a movement of nationalistic aspirations under which concepts of change and modernization are loaded with ideological meanings. In this form change ceases to be viewed as a normal social process, it is transferred into an ideology than change in itself desirable and must be sought for."[50]

The very purpose of traditional philosophy in India is often not only suspected but questioned. This is because a large number of books are available on Indian philosophy by the native as well as foreign writers but their interpretations widely differ. There is a category of books on Indian philosophy written by a single author or in collaboration which not only explain but also analyse the theories and teachings of thinkers, sages and also philosophers which cover ancient and modern periods. However, efforts have not been made to trace the modern Indian renaissance in certain movements. An account of Sri Ramkrishna Paramhansa about whom Romain Rolland has said that he was "the consummation of two thousand years of the spiritual life of three hundred million people", is not included but the teachings of his chief apostle Swami Vivekananda find a place. It may partly be due to the neo-Vedantic style adopted by the latter to suit the demands of the modern world.

Moreover, perhaps they thought that if traditional philosophies are subjected to a rational analysis they might not fulfil the minimum expectations. One of the main reasons was the short lived purpose of most of the traditional philosophies. The purpose of the traditional philosophy is well illustrated in the following words: "The primary aim of the traditional philosophy is an individual interpretation but a good many philosophers might agree that it is a fair description of one important function of philosophy in the past. Now this aim of traditional philosophy has come to be mistrusted for the following reason. If a belief is to be rationally justified it must satisfy certain criteria. It is consistency and the means of testing this, is logic, the chief tool of the philosopher. But consistency alone is not enough, to make a belief or set of beliefs, rationally accepted."[51]

Unlike traditional philosophy in the West, the classical traditions in India have been deeply rooted in the soil than elsewhere. Therefore, even the contemporary Indian philosophers are bound to be influenced by the mill of the traditional philosophy. The influence of traditional philosophy in India is greater than the influence of pragmatism in America, or empiricism in Britain, or idealistic and pessimistic attitude in Germany.

As such, it is essential for all the traditional philosophies whether eastern or western to undertake the prescribed logical test and to a certain extent prove its pragmatic utility. This would certainly help arrive at some conclusion. It has become an inherent tendency to accept values at their superficial level, without taking into consideration the conscious reasoning. We believe in the mass opinion and setting aside the past traditions, are prepared to readjust it, for the sake of necessity. Moreover, certain problems of tradition are deliberately neglected, as they are considered to be inevitable. Therefore, it can be said that to build up a new theory or form new ideals, would be unreasonable. Similarly, there is much truth in the following statement: "The idea that ancient knew everything and there is nothing new to be now discovered, especially in the department of ethics and social science, is one that can never be accepted by a rationalist."[52]

In fact, the status of Indian philosophy is predetermined by the general Indian temperament. A glance at the development of Indian philosophy shows that is is a continuous process. It does not have broken links to be united. This is because it never appeared to have confusion at any stage. On the other hand, it gives the impression of being very analytical at every stage. This has been mistaken for treading through confusion or groping in darkness. The fact is that consulting the past for erecting faultless and needed philosophies, had been a regular practice. This may be viewed as a very typical of Indian tradition because though it had continuous onslaught of materialism in past yet it did not allow any such wave to weaken its character.

Besides, it is said: "Reverence for the past is another national trait. There is certain doggedness of temperament, a stubborn loyalty to lose nothing in the long march of the ages. When confronted with new cultures or sudden extensions of knowledge, the Indian does not yield to the tradition of the hour, but holds fast to his traditional faith, importing as much as possible of the new into the old. This conservative liberalism is the secret of success of Indian culture and civilization."[53]

Therefore, loosening of the old traditional bonds is also not in the vicinity of usual probabilities. Since they have to be conserved, at the most, their form could be changed but the essence or spirit has to be retained. For this no civilization or culture could stand exception.

NOTES AND REFERENCES

1. The Content of Cultural Continuity in India, Journal of Asian Studies, Vol. XX, No.4, Aug. 61, p. 434.
2. Religion and Progress in Modern Asia, Ed. R.N. Bellah, pp. 170-171.
3. M.N. Srinivas, The Nature of the Problem of Indian Unity, p.105.
4. Dictionary of Philosophy, Ed. I. Frolor, p.247.
5. Micropaedia Britannica Vol. X, p. 85.
6. Ct, Modernization of Indian Tradition, Yogendra Singh, p.23.
7. Louis Dumont, Contributions, p.12.
8. Lucille Schullberg, Historic India, p.113.

9. Eastern Mysticism, Vol. I, Ed. Raymond Van Over, p.41.
10. Sources of Indian Tradition, Compiled Wm. Theodore de Bary et al., p.104.
11. A Dictionary of Philosophy, Ed. Antony Flew, p.247.
12. Bishop Whitehead, Indian Philosophy, p.3..
13. Debiprasad Chattopadhayaya, Indian Philosophy: Popular Introduction, p.6.
14. A Source Book in Indian Philosophy, Ed. S. Radhakrishnan and Charles A. Moore, General Introduction, p. xxviii.
15. P. Ramamurthi, The Problem of Indian Polity, p.32.
16. P.T. Raju, The Philosophical Traditions of India, pp. 14, 15.
17. S. Radhakrishnan, Indian Philosophy, op. cit., p.24.
18. Charles Eliot, Hinduism and Buddhism, Vol. II, p.166.
19. P. Ramamurthi, The Problem of Indian Polity, p.24.
20. Hiriyanna, Outlines of Indian Philosophy, p.17.
21. S. Radhakrishnan, Indian Philosophy, op. cit., pp. 46-47.
22. Fleming H. Revell, An Interpretation of India's Religious History, p. 164.
23. D. S. Sarma, Hinduism Through the Ages, p.1.
24. Yogendra Singh, Modernization of Indian Tradition, p.88.
25. Karl H. Potter, Presupositions of India's Philosophies, p.2.
26. *Ibid.*, p.3.
27. Charles A. Moore, The Indian Mind, p.12.
28. Hiriyanna, Outlines of Indian Philosophy, op. cit., p.17.
29. J. Sinha, Introduction to Philosophy, p. 16.
30. S.V. Venkateshwara, Indian Culture Through the Ages, p. 32.
31. Dhirendra M. Datta, The Chief Currents of Contemporary Philosophy, p. 578.
32. S. Radhakrishnan, Indian Philosophy, p. 32.
33. P. T. Raju, The Philosophical Traditions of India, Introduction.
34. *Ibid.*
35. Igor Naletor P., Alternatives to Positivism, p. 25.
36. *Ibid.*, p. 28.
37. Some European Parallels in Buddhistic Logic, Vol. I, p. 529.
38. *Ibid.*, p. 546.
39. V. Brodor, Indian Philosophy, p. 30.
40. Frank Thilly, A History of Philosophy, p. 7.
41. *Ibid.*, p. 3.
42. S. Radhakrishnan, Indian Philosophy, pp. 24, 25.
43. P. Ramamurthy, The Problem of Indian Polity, pp. 28-29.
44. Dasgupta, History of Indian Philosophy, p.1.
45. Rudolph and Rudolph, The Modernity of Tradition, p. 3.

46. Robert Hume, Interpretation of India's Religious History, p. 164.
47. Max Muller, The Six Systems of Indian Philosophy, p. 370.
48. A. C. Underwood, Contemporary Thought, p. 3.
49. Rudolph and Rudolph, The Modernity of Tradition, p. 5.
50. Louis Dumont Contributions, op. cit., Introduction.
51. *Ibid.*
52. Paranjpe - Kamala Lectures.
53. Philosophies of India, Henrich Zimmer, p. 48.

2

Traditions in the Vedic and Post-Vedic Periods

To describe Vedic scriptures with certainty under a specific period of history is a difficult task. Various historians opine that they must have been spread over a long period when recorded. Therefore, the period lying between 1500 B.C. and 800 B.C. is usually accepted. Since Vedas were held in great esteem by the Hindus, most of the traditions seemed to have emerged out of them. The Vedas are supposed to reveal the eternal truths and as such they do command unquestionable authority. They are regarded the fountainhead of all wisdom with limitless scope. The orthodox Hindus consider Vedas as divine.

In this regard, H. Bhattacharya opines, "The Hindus trace the original source of their cultural life to the Vedas which they hold to be divine truths, revealed from time to time to the Rsis, seers, in their supernomal consciousness. Their religion, philosophy, ritualistic practices, civic conduct and even social relations are guided by certain codes which are known as Smritis but all of them are based upon the sacred sanction of Vedic authority. Even the Itihasas, Puranas are to be read as commentaries on the sacred Vedas. Manu, the greatest law-giver, of India has explicitly stated that these should be considered as an elaboration of the Vedas. It is a recognized rule of procedure that whenever there seems to be a difference between the Sruti (the Vedas) and the Smriti, the Sruti has been upheld as the supreme authority and the Smriti has to be interpreted in consonance with it. No school of philosophy will be recognized as orthodox, if it is not supported by the authority of the Vedas.

The whole life of a Hindu, from conception to the last funeral rites has to be sanctified by the recitation of Vedic mantras (sacred text). From these facts it may easily be conceived how profound has been the influence of the Vedas upon this great and most ancient of the civilized nations of the world."[1]

In order to understand the Vedic scriptures, it is necessary to give a brief account of Vedas. There are four Vedas, viz., Rg Veda, Sama Veda, Yajur Veda and Atharva Veda. Each one has four recognized components, named as the Samhitas, the Brahmanas, the Aranyakas and the Upanisads. The first three deal with the rituals and sanctions while the last one lays stress only on knowledge which is to some extent impinged upon by the philosophical fetters and very often shows the signs of being transcendental. In short, the Samhitas, are hymns composed in praise of various Nature-Gods with a view to receive benedictions for material prosperity. The Brahmanas provide proper methods for the performance of the accepted rituals. ceremonies and to a certain extent they lay down the rigid codes of human conduct.

S. Radhakrishnan observes: "The Brahmans are manuals for performing various kinds of rituals and ceremonies as well as guides for the conduct of every day life. They describe in detail, procedures for performing different rituals for pleasing different gods as well as the kinds of sacrifices to be offered to them."[2]

There is no denying the fact they Rg Veda has been regarded as the oldest Indo-European literary and philosophical movement. Vedas in all their forms represent wisdom. In fact, the sages of the Vedic period were very often obsessed with questions which are at present construed as partly religious and partly philosophical. It seems that abstract metaphysics played a dominant role at that time. The writings were poetic and therefore, an element of mysticism was something inevitable. Since the Indian thought is largely based upon the Vedic spirit and because of its rigorous polytheistic attitudes various questions related to the philosophical character cropped up from time to time. The following few questions well-illustrate this: "What God shall we adore with our oblation? Who can have declare where it was born and whence comes this creation? The Gods are later than this world's production? Who knows whence it first came into being?"[3]

The Vedic literature is not entirely free from atheistic objections. There had been inquiries regarding the very existence of God and also about the nature of God. Such queries were made by the Vedic sages due to which one cannot rule out the possibility of the beginning of the scientific temperament. This shows that a close examination of the Rg Veda cannot be dispensed with for a thorough understanding of the Indian thought.

Therefore, though the opposite tendencies were given their due consideration, yet they could not form a substantial theory to override the sound doctrines which Vedic literature could boast of. It is however, necessary to note such deviations, the rules of conduct and duties of men towards each other.

The Vedas consist of hymns and treatises which throw light on the intellectural plane of comprehension of the early Aryan people. In fact, they are the honestly written manuals of Aryan experiences. Since they are constituted in essence by a noteworthy spiritual excellence, they continue to command respect even today. The mystics of India purveyed Vedas with their intuitive experiences, which indeed helped the earliest documents of the Aryans to bring forth a literature with authenticity. Thus the intuitive thoughts and the subsequent judgements, served a useful purpose.

As Sri Aurobindo points out: "In the fixed tradition of thousands of years they have been revered as origin and standard of all that can be held as authoritative and true in Brahmana and Upanisad, the Tantra and Purana, in the doctrines of great philosophical schools and in the teachings of famous saints and sages".[4]

One of the central themes of Vedas that can easily be pointed out is projecting of the lofty truths of life and life after death. It is important to note that the latter is treated as a riddle of life and a problem of practical philosophy. Therefore, the Vedic traditions advanced in all the later spiritual movements and attained a philosophical grandeur. Nevertheless, it was inevitable for the Vedas to erect more or less a religious philosophy at its substratum than a purely classical philosophy. For Hindus the roots of their cultural heritage and traditions have to be traced from the Vedic time alone. This does not mean that the Indian philosophers had not challenged the authority of Vedas. However, it is generally held that the Indian philosophy never faced such situations but for the efforts of Western scholars who suggested certain corrective measures. In the words of S. Radhakrishnan: "Whatever we may think of them, half formed myths or crude allegories, obscure gropings or immature compositions, still they are the source of the later practices and philosophies of the Indo-Aryans and a study of them is necessary for a proper understanding of subsequent thought."[5] A.C. Bose makes this more clearly when he points out : "We do not find in the Vedas any evidence of the tragedy of the divided soul and the anguish and misery that accompany it (as we find among the Greeks). Nor do we come across signs of repression or self-torture, accompanying by morbid sin-consciousness, sometimes found... among followers of the Hebraic religions. No negative attitude induced by dis-illusionment..., no world weariness is in evidence in the Vedas. Vedic sages are positive in their acceptance of life and death...of the ultimate values of truth, goodness, beauty - and the eternal law Rta..."[6]

This indicates that due to over-enthusiasm, the interpretation of Vedic literature caused a great damage as it presented the pessimistic view of the world. This is obvious from the fact that while describing the theory of illusion, its scope and mortality of the organic objects, the commentators have painted a depressive picture of the world. In fact, the rsis experienced an element of spirituality and discipline in it and as such they propogated their experience. They felt the necessity of understanding every mystical experience which they had in this physical universe. In view of this, it is wrong to believe that the Vedic traditions were not concerned with the physical universe and their advocates remained indifferent to the beauty and joy of life. It is remarked: "The visions of the beauty of life and nature in the Vedas are extremely rich in poetic value. Perhaps no where in the world has the glory of dawn and sunrise and the silence and sweetness of nature received such rich and at the same time such pure expression."[7]

Amongst the four Vedas, Rg Veda is considered as the oldest literary and philosophical monument. The Vedic sages were desperately trying to find out solutions for various philosophical inquiries and riddles. This is apparent from the Upanisads which teem with several philosophical speculations. The roots of many schools of Indian philosophy established later on, were found in the Upanisads. In view of this, it is necessary to explain the real significance of the Upanisads. Bishop in 'Indian Thought' points out:

"It is to the credit of Upanisadic thinkers that for the first time in the history of Indian philosophy, philosophical thinking seems to have been consciously and purposely undertaken in the Upanisads. Though the Upanisads thus mark the beginning of philosophizing in India the philosophy they have produced is not to be considered crude. We find that the subtlety with which problems are raised and answered in the Upanishads is remarkable."[8]

As far as the continuity of the Vedic traditions is concerned, it can be said that there are only five philosophical systems which could be considered as the real offshoots of them. They categorically held Vedas as the only infallible source of knowledge and authority. This, however, does not mean that they are derivative and devoid of originality. It is true that in Vedanta or Upanisads there is an inherent tendency to claim systematisation of the philosophical knowledge contained in Vedas. Mimamsa very often played the role of defending Vedic standpoint and subsequently the literature therein.

Surprisingly, Mimamsa has strived to liberate itself from the classical orthodox system of Indian philosophy. Nevertheless while doing this it has neither expressed the weighty orthodox postulates nor atheistic attitudes. It remained indifferent to the question of the existence of God. Of course today many scholars have tried to show that Mimamsa never went under the belt of atheism; On the other hand it was typically theistic. As it is observed: "Feeble and quite fanciful efforts are sometimes made by the modern scholars to prove that this orthodox philosophy par excellence could not be atheistic."[9]

In fact, this issue still remains unresolved as modern scholars hold different opinions. Some of them plead that except for the denial of God, this theory has no other weakness. As such, even with regard to the constitution of the phenomena of the world and its functioning, the opinions differ. Referring to this blatant objection, S. Radhakrishnan opines; "This lacuna of Purva Mimamsa was so unsatisfactory that the later writers slowly smuggled in God."[10]

Approach to Vedanta

From the very beginning in India religion had tended to dominate almost all the systems of philosophy. Therefore, it can be said that most of the common activities of the multifaceted culture are nothing but manoeuvring of religious bent. It is said: "Religion is not an independent phenomenon in India. Religion is not conceived as a duty or a problem facing every human being on reaching maturity. It is a heritage and a tradition. It is not an obsession of the human mind as it is constantly asserted."[11]

Therefore, despite a number of transition stages, at every point the culture has been elongating without any strain or discard. In other words, it has attained maturity to such an extent that long back it had begun transcending. As far as the system of Vedanta is concerned, it can be said that it has Absolutistic and Theistic approaches. The Absolutistic approach was adopted by Sankara as Advaita philosophy. While Theistic approach was adopted by Ramanuja as Visistadvaita. There are some more recognized approaches but the philosophy of the Upanisads is the philosophy of the two schools which totally differ. Each of them, viz., the monistic and the theistic claim, the true following is achieved only by it. This cannot be considered as something very new because though the subject is spiritual, the deal was in the hands of human beings. The temperamental differences and needs have worked in an unusually spirited way as it happened in the cultural history of many nations. As ever, the battle for supremacy became inevitable. Even then unlike anywhere only in Upanisads one can find the power of self-renewal. It is worth noting that the doctrine of Vedanta is derived from the triple texts: The Upanisads, The Bhagwad Gita and Vedanta Sutra. Since the Vedantic literature forms the concluding portion of the Vedas it embodies metaphysical doctrines and visions of the ancient sages of India. Therefore, it can at anytime undergo the test of logic. A comparison of both shows that the Purva Mimamsa schools is the outcome of the ritualistic part of the Vedic tradition or culture. Similarly Uttara Mimamsa or Vedanta has been the sign of development of its speculative part.

The Vedantic Tradition

Needless to say, the Vedanta systematically presents its philosophy and has close bearing on the orthodox religious spirit of India. On the one hand, Purva Mimamsa mainly relies upon the knowledge, especially Vedas, for the active side of life. It attaches much significance to the workability of the rhetorical design. On the other hand Uttara Mimamsa encourages all possible religious and philosophical speculations of the

Upanisads. On the whole both together display the spirit of Veda and thereby give rise to the emergence of Vedic traditions.

The Vedanta Sutra also known as Brahma Sutra is closely connected with the doctrine of Vedanta. Therefore, in order to understand it, it is necessary to refer to the commentaries of philosophers, particularly of the ancient times. The Sutras are not sketchy nevertheless their interpretations invariably differ. This is because they have been written in a subtle manner. In fact, there are number of Sutras, i.e., five hundred and fifty five as such the commentaries over them vary in style. Among the major commentators, mention may be made of Sankara, Ramanuja and Madhava.

It is of course, very difficult to speak in detail of any religion without offending certain old beliefs. Moreover, certain philosophical aspects of the religion are so sacred that scientific analysis of them is highly difficult if not impossible. Efforts had been made in this regard but, they were misdirected and proved to be futile. In fact, there are halucinations, growing tissues of errors which continued to dominate as they remained unchecked and were sanctified by theoretical principles.

Another obstacle that came in the path of Indian philosophy was the mythological explanation of the world. This difficulty was also, faced by other countries but they could overcome this by releasing self. Scriptures and legends have been intermingled with the then existing philosophical speculation. This is obvious from the fact that Green in Prolegomena to Ethics (p. 99) and Bradley in Appearance and Reality (p. 453), indicate or rather openly confess that the why and how of creation cannot be explained by philosophy. Similarly, Sankara, the Advaita philosopher also does not pretend to know the world merely with the assistance of philosophical speculations. There are, likewise, certain discrepancies which really need to be pointed. The Upanisadic connection with Vedas, as explained by Marxists, well illustrates this: "The traditional claim is that the Upanisads are parts of the Veda. It is however, necessary to note that in the Vedic tradition itself the idealistic outlook of the Upanisads meant a decisive break with the ancestral convictions. This was virtually admitted in some of the passages of the Upanisads wherein Narada, e.g., is found seeking the knowledge of the self in spite of possessing the knowledge of the Vedas. The first thing he was told by Sanatakumara was that, among other branches of knowledge, the Rgveda, the Yajurveda, the Sama Veda and the Atharva Veda as the fourth were 'mere names'. Evidently, it was felt that something new-something other than what was contained in the early compilations was needed. Evidently, again, the need was felt because of a new situation."[12]

Sankara's Non-dulism

It is interesting to note that Sankara's Advaita theory is nothing but a replica of the statements in Vedas. However, he claims to have presented the Vedic doctrines in a new format. Of course, it is true that he firmly represents one of the best aspects from the Vedic philosophy which later on led to the establishment of an exclusive school of thought. This theory mainly concentrates on doubts about the knowledge of the empirical world. It is very difficult to know the world entirely as the Surfacial or phenomenal part of it differs in appearance and reality. Sankara does not attach any importance to a knowledge derived from the dictates of our senses and memory. He holds that although illusory knowledge apparently appears to be the most genuine one, it is always liable to be faulty. He asserts that the illusions are so strong that it is difficult to achieve real knowledge without getting into the details of them. He tries to emphasize that most of our experiences, ideas and feelings can be considered as the spell of an illusory note only. Despite this, he opines that the very existence of 'self' is beyond doubt. As pointed out: "All means of knowledge exist only as dependent on self-experience and since such experience is its own proof there is no necessity for proving the existence of self."[13]

Sankara has evaluated 'self' in an unconventional manner, i.e., trying to establish the supremacy without providing a paradigm of qualities. As he has chosen self as everything and yet with separate identity, the usual question of its existence or dimensions in particular does not arise. One of the essential and self generating qualities of it is that it is not pointed by the empirical world. This is because most of things are under the chain of the phenomenal values. While disregarding the empirical world, he goes to the extent of declaring the world as an illusory stage and can never be the ultimate relaity. Thus, although his theory is logically consistent, it is nothing but a theory of negation devoid of any optimism. Nonetheless it is rightly pointed out: "It is not that Sankara paints gloomy picture of the world by displaying only its severe limitations and man's incapacity. He suggests a release from the same by way of devotion and self realisation. This attainment is not 'The dissolution of the world but is the displacement of a false outlook (avidya) by the right outlook wisdom (vidya)".[14]

According to Sankara it is necessary to distinguish two different attitudes. They are the ordinary or empirical and real or transcendental. The former continues to dwell in the domain of ignorance and considers it as the only possible world. The latter can be regarded as enlightened one because it dispels ignorance. The unenlightened one considers the world as real one and therefore, it is called Vyavaharika point of view or a practical one. One account of this various qualities like omnipotence, omniscience, omnipresence appear to be qualifications of God who is hence called Saguna Brahman or Isvara. The enlightened one realises that the world is a mere appearance. Contrary to the claims of the empirical philosophers, God is totally bereft of any qualities as he ceases to be regarded as any real creator. This type of attitude points God as without the characteristics which in fact, are supposed to be essential for a all-powerful God. Thus he becomes Nirguna. Although Sankara clarifies both, the attributed and attributeless viewpoints, he is not prepared to accept the world as complementary to the God of either type. He also does not indicate the possible conjugation of these two. In view of this, it can be said that Sankara's theory of God has a rational basis. According to him: "(i) Pure existence is the ground and material of all particular and changing forms of existence constituting the world, (ii) That particular objects being open to contradiction cannot be taken as absolutely real, (iii) That only pure existence is beyond actual and possible contradiction and therefore, the only absolute reality, (iv) That pure existence is pure consciousness as well."[15]

Therefore, what has been consistently stressed here is the fact that the Absolute existence is itself God and both the forms, immanent and transcendental can be deduced logically. It is only when the critical examination is done then the acceptance of reality through world is ruled out.

Sankara and Spinoza

Both Sankara and Spinoza are sometimes accused of atheism in its popular sense. This is because though Spinoza's conception of God is substance which differs from Sankara's Nirguna Brahman yet both concepts are different from the concept of God found in various religions. In fact, both attempt to find out the supreme reality in God. Sankara and Spinoza alike try to over-discipline the usual theistic approach. That is to say as atheism concentrates on the empirical world and its experiences and does not even care to think of the different possibility of the existence of God, similarly, theism focusses its attention to both, the world and its controller God. The atheism of the past and that of today differ on many counts. The present day atheism is pregnant with agnosticism, skepticism etc. Therefore, not only the existence of God but also the nature of the God are not easily accepted. In view of this, it is necessary to take into consideration the period while making the assessment of the atheistic position of the philosopher.

Sankara clearly states his view regarding theism in which the world does not stand any chance for a belief. He asserts his firm faith only in God. This view is generally regarded as neither theistic nor atheistic but supertheistic. As it it said: "This points to the stage where love of God becomes absolute, suffering neither ego nor the world. If this type of faith is to be distinguished from ordinary theism (or belief in personal God) the word for it should be not theism, but rather Supertheism."[16]

It can be said that Sankara does not simply explain the world but explains it away. This may be regarded as one of the serious dreawbacks in the spirit of philosophical studies as philosophy is supposed to explain the world. From this point of view Sankara's philosophy appears to be full of contradictions and therefore, it can not be relied upon. Since Sankara's theory rarely keeps pace with the practical aspect of life, it may at best be considered as unworldly or other-wordly. If this theory is examined with practical approach, it seems to be over-speculative or idealistic and the world loses all its meaning. Logically, a deletion of the world from the theory requires proper explanation.

Thus, Sankara's philosophy has been subjected to a good deal of criticism. A close scrutiny of it shows the Upanisadic idea of unity of all existence has led Sankara's philosophy to concentrate on God. Despite all these defects, Sankara's philosophy should not be underestimated since it is considered as the most consistent system of monism in the history of human thought.

While speaking high about Sankara's Vedanta as presented by Vivekananda in America, William James points out: "The paragon of all monistic system is the Vedanta philosophy of Hindustan".[17] It seems that due to its unidirectional sight regarding the location of every detail of the world, this system fails to attract those who are keen either to rectify or re-assess the worldly values. It is welcomed by those who follow the spiritual path or have a yearning for spiritual discipline in life or find consolation not in anything else except in monism. For them, Advaita monism guarantees the emotional security and satisfaction.

While explaining the theories, i.e., Advaita, Davaita, Visistadvaita which even today are life and blood of the Indian philosophy, William James opines: "An Absolute one and I that one surely we have a religion which emotionally considered, has a high pragmatic value; it imparts a perfect sumptuousity of security." "We all have some ear for this monistic music; it elevates and reassures."[18]

Ramanuja's Qualified Non-Dualism

Ramanuja's philosophy comprises concepts of world, Self and God. Unlike Sankara, Ramanuja has not focussed his entire attention on God. Although his philosophy holds God at the helm and considers the world and self as complementary, however, he insists that the latter are as important as God because they are also real. However, Ramanuja indirectly elevates the status of God by declaring the dependency of the world and self on God. While describing 'Brahman' he gives importance to all the qualities leading to perfection and the common traps likely to induce imperfection are abhorred. That is to say 'Brahman' is considered to be absolutely free from any kind of imperfection or even momentary disturbance in discipline. The different levels of consciousness do not include matter as according to Ramanuja, matter is never conscious. As far as individual selves are concerned they are prone to sufferings. In order to get rid of sufferings one must dispel ignorance and subsequently get freedom from the bondage.

Thus, it can be said that though Ramanuja gives a different picture of 'Reality' still he concentrates on Brahman only and gives him the highest status. The existence of World and Selves have been recognised but they have not been given the similar status. Brahman is supposed to have the governing power over the rest of the people. Even the complementary status given to the world and self, becomes meaningless without reference to Brahman. Since philosophies of both Sankara and Ramanuja emphasise the non-dualistic approach, one is likely to get the impression that there is no sharp distinction between them. In fact, Ramanuja cautions by stating that the self may be released from ignorance by attaining knowledge but that may not be a right path to become one with the God. This is because although salvation is guaranteed by virtues of knowledge nevertheless it can not bridge the gap between life and God and the self. Both Sankara and. Ramanuja admit that man has no existence independent of God but they interpret this dependence of self on God in a different manner. As it is pointed out: 'Ramanuja takes the Upanisadic accounts of creation in a literal sense. He holds that God who is omnipotent creates the manifold world out of himself by gracious act of will. Within All-inclusive God (Brahman) there are both unconscious matter and finite spirits. The first is the source of the material objects and as such called Prakriti... whose authority Ramanuja highly values... During the state of dissolution this primal unconscious nature of Prakriti remains in a latent, subtle and undifferentiated form. God creates out of this, the world of diverse objects in accordance with the deeds of the souls in the world prior to the last dissolution. Impelled by omnipotent will of God the undifferentiated subtle matter gradually becomes transformed into three kinds of subtle elements - fire, water and earth.

Ramanuja holds, therefore, that creation is a fact and the created world is as real as Brahman. Regarding the Upanisadic texts which deny the multiplicity of objects and asserts the unity of all things Ramnuja holds that these texts do not mean to deny the reality of many objects but to teach that in all of them there is the same Brahman, on which all are dependent for existence.[19]

There are certain basic differences between philosophies of Ramanuja and Sankara. Ramanuja is considered to be as very systematic interpretor of theistic Vedanta. His approach is contrary to that of Sankara. It is believed that Ramanuja's Visistadvaita is composed of different texts and also some of the mystical writings of the ancient time. His arguments are grounded on Upanisads. Therefore, when it is said that neither the mind nor speech can describe Brahman it does not mean that the

Brahman is absolutely unknowable. It only mean that with all our stock of ideas, knowledge and feelings, we can have partial knowledge of the Lord. This is due to our limited perception. As P. Nagarja Rao in 'Introduction to Vedanta' writes: "The fundamental authority for Ramanuja's conception of Ultimate Reality is the Upanisads. The roots of Ramanuja's monotheism can be traced back to the Vedas. In the Upanisads there is a warm current of theism and a personalistic conception of Reality. Supreme Reality is described as Narayana. He is referred to as being immanent and also transcendent. He is referred to as the creator, sustainer, and destroyer of the world."[20]

According to Ramanuja it is essential to clarify the position of man with respect to God as described in the Upanisads. Since man is finite it is not possible to equate him with God in every respect. Therefore when it is argued that man is not different from God, it means that God pervades and controls man as every other thing in the Universe. The very existence of man is not possible without God. The fabrication of world is possible only by recognizing man and God. However, none can have a status without reference to the other. Thus, on the one hand Ramanuja considers the phenomenal world as a real to the extent of Brahman. On the other hand, Sankara holds that the phenomenal world cannot be real; at the most it can remain a mere appearance. Whatever, their views may be, it can be said that since no status is given to the world, it can be regarded neither real nor unreal. Sankara and Ramanuja also differ in their conception of knowledge. This is well illustrated by the following statement:

"Sankara recognizes two kinds of knowledge (consciousness): the lower governed by the distinctions between the knower, the known, and the act of knowing and the higher, which transcends these distinctions. According to Sankara, knowledge of the empirical world is subject to the above distinctions, whereas knowledge of Brahman is itself pure Being, Pure consciousness, and Pure Bliss. Ramanuja on the other hand, holds that knowledge analytically implies the knower and the known and hence cannot be identified with the knower or the known; where there is no knower, there can be nothing to be known either consequently, argues Ramanuja, experience of reality is not an experience in which the self, non-self distinction is obliterated, but on which the self-becomes conscious of the unity of reality."[21]

On the basis of the above facts, it can safely be said that Ramanuja's philosophy not only opposes Sankara's philosophy with regard to the popular concepts like knowledge, Reality, World, Maya, Brahman but also provides a scientific outlook which goes to a large extent to convince the modern mind. It is difficult to understand any theory, which is entirely based on metaphysics and is subtle in its expression, particularly when it ignores the phenomenal world. Thus Ramanuja's non-dualism has been influenced by his great teachers (Acharyaas) and also poet-saints (alvars) who ruled out the possibility of philosophical aridity.

Madhava's Dualism

Madhava also upholds the view that God, Selves and the World have permanent existence. Nonetheless, he attempts to point out in his philosophy that God is something unique and as such the selves and the World are subordinate to him. Since we draw a clean distinction between them his dualism is undoubtedly accepted. God is viewed as the ultimate in perfection and governing the other two. Everything that exists on this planet is regarded as a living organism. Like other philosophers, Madhava holds that the virtues and vices are the outcome of one's own misdeeds committed in the earlier life. This naturally leads him to admit the theory of rebirth. In fact, the theory of rebirth and its presuppositions have been neither denied nor discussed separately by other philosophers. Besides, the principles of Hindu religion and philosophies of ancient time very often went hand in hand and, provided a mixed result thereby certain concepts had been emerged.

Nevertheless as far as Madhava's philosophy is concerned it is difficult to explain his approach to God. According to him God cannot be approached directly. 'Vayu' is considered to be the mediator. It is the Divine Will, which always directs the course of life. It may drive us into a bondage or even liberate from it. Thus God is the supreme and has no control over the happenings. It is God who makes or marks the destiny of everyone. Hence in view of Madhava worship is the only way through which we can commune with God.

Besides, Dvaita Vedanta (Dualism) as the name itself indicates, rejects all the earlier non-dualistic concepts; whether they belong to Sankara or Ramanuja. It lays great emphasis on the thorough going of dualism between the world and Brahman. The philosophic foundation of Madhava's theory can be grasped only by studying in detail his views on perception and knowledge. According to Madhava to perceive an object is to gain knowledge or to become aware of it. A study of the different schools of Indian thought shows that the concept of divine grace was held in great esteem. This is essentially so in case of old religious literature which contains the doctrine of grace. The doctrine of grace which leads to man's true liberation has emerged through those theistic schools. The intensity of grace to be conceived goes proportionately with the human operation and endeavour. They in fact serve a condition, though they alone are not capable of bringing out the desired results.

As far as the highest type of Bhakti is concerned it is based on knowledge and nothing else. Madhava opines that it could sprout only when the majesty of God is completely recognized. This is technically called Mahatyma-Jnanapurva). Thus, although Madhava's views are different from those of Sankara and Ramanuja, they are not subject to the emotional and ritualistic aberrations, which normally oozes out of the popular sentiment of Bhakti. This becomes clear when Mahdva's Dvaita is interpreted from the metaphysical point of view. "Madhava, while an Advaita Vedantin, presents a Dvaiti interpretation. According to him ultimate Reality is Brahman whom he calls Vishnu or Hari, who is self-existent, subsistent and dependent, every other thing being dependent on it. Brahman is the same as God who is omnipresent, all pervading and possessing infinite qualities since he is innermost reality and cause of everything. He is devoid of qualities (Nirguna) but becomes many yet still remains one without any defect or contamination."[22]

Apart from this description we have also Madhava delineated as a dualist with certain exclusive qualities which attach lot of importance. "Madhava is a dualist because he believes differences and distinctions in the world are real. In fact, he is not a dualist but a Bhedavadin who asserts there are the five real distinctions between God and souls, one soul and another God and matter, soul and matter and one object and another."[23]

Though Madhava accepts the reality of difference yet he prefers to remain a monist. This need not be considered as self-contradictory, because he trusts in the ultimate reality and accepts that as only one. This he calls God, to whom the best qualities are labelled. He is also, in view of Madhava the impeller of all actions. Madhava also declares that the above stated five types of differences are permanent, in the sense, external. Therefore, they will never disappear. Coexistence of individual souls and matter which God, is a basic condition. Therefore, the differences are bound to remain as they are. At the end Madhava proposes yet another view of the souls and their capacity. To him souls do possess the qualities, necessary for them to be easily characterised but in a limited fashion. They hold bliss knowledge and power, but within a given scope. This is because of the rule of Karma. Many a time, the souls are masked by the very Karma of ignorance. Therefore, all their actions, knowledge, ignorance, bondage and deliverence are caused by God in accordance with their Karmas. The soul has two aspects, the intrinsic and immutable, and the external and mutable. Second one has the physical plane wherein, senses, mind and temporary qualities preside. Everything, qualitywise remain in the transitory state. Probably it is the ignorance which makes to them remain at the latent phase. Therefore, the soul finds freedom only when it can liberate itself from such transient extensive qualities. What has been commonly recommended is also true for Madhava, i.e., surrender to the omnipotent God to receive his grace. It is that state wherein nothing can touch, or influence the soul. The state is described in own exclusive way by different religions. What is important is an outright rejection of the extensive qualities and adherence to the intensive ones.

Thus, is can be said that Madhava's philosophy oscillates between the advaitic ideal and dvaitic reasoning of the world, soul and God. He recognises the existence of all these objects which are independent but classifies them on the basis of their capacity and qualities. The point of opposition might indicate Madhava's genius at differentiating the intensive and extensive qualities but then, that was essential for a complete theory or philosophy.

The Vedanta of Nimbarka

Nimbarka's philosophy is based on the Vaisnava tradition, which lays great stress on the path of devotion. Nimbarka, who presented a new conception of the relation between the all pervading Brahman and the soul (atman) along with the material world, as a philosophy of the tenth century. Nimbarka's argument deserves a special attention in the philosophical traditions of India in the post Vedic period because his theory springs from the essentials of Sankara's and Madhava's philosophies. In fact, these two philosophers held quite contrary views. Sankara adhered to the non-difference theory while Madhava emphasised the theory of absolute difference with regard to the relation between Brahman, soul, and material world. According to Nimbarka, a golden mean of these rival theories is necessary and therefore, he suggested that a complex relation of identity (abheda)—difference (bheda) has to be accepted. Therefore, it is better to accept this typical relation by designating it is identity in difference just as we speak of cultures as unity in diversity. In fact, Ramanuja was the first philosopher who pointed out this and suggested a reconciliation between identity and difference. Nevertheless, he did not want this blending by unifying them but initially to reject both of them and then to present a new concrete form of body soul relationship.

Thus, Nimbarka's philosophy is based on scientific analysis as it takes into consideration the cause and effect of the problem and relates the solution of it with the identity and difference relation. He pointed out the similarities as well as differences between the Brahman, the soul and the material world.

The Activist Tradition

The activist tradition is mainly concerned with philosophies which deem 'activism' as the summum bonum of life, and the ultimate reality. Hence, it can be said that every experience of life is nothing but a process of activity. Nevertheless, it is important to note that the Indian philosophers who subscribed to this tradition do not have agreement on the doctrine and everyone expresses his own views regarding the term 'activity'. This ultimately led to the emergence of various concepts of activity. For example, Nirukta which means Sanskrit lexicon, provides general meanings of difficult words contained in Vedas. On account of this, we refer to the school of Nairuktas or lexiconists. According to this school, Atman or Soul is the sole reality while everything else is only a shade or form of it. In fact, it is not a new concept but derived from some of the Vedantic philosophies. Nevertheless, it differs as far as the nature of Atman as a pure activity, involved in an uninterrupted process is concerned. They mainly relied on the Vedic languages because it was the only language which could help them to know the nature of reality. This is obvious from the fact that the philosophers who stick to grammarian discipline held: 'Atman or Soul alone is real and since the Atman is pure activity, the verb, which expresses activity in any sentence, is the primary part of the sentence. And just as everything else in the universe is only a mode of the Atman, which is activity itself, all the other parts of the sentence the subject, the object, etc., —are only modes of the verb. So in interpreting the Vedas, the Nairuktas say, we should take the words denoting activity as primary and the rest as secondary..."[24]

Another kind of interpretation was given by the Mimamsakas. Nevertheless, unlike Nairuktas, the Mimamsakas did not hold Atman as synonym to Activity. They relied upon the Activity principle as they believed it controls the functioning of the Universe. However, Mimamsakas did not agree on equating Activity to the Universe. Thus, it appears that Mimamsakas adopted the scientific principle in order to overcome the lacuna found in the Niruktas. According to them, activity is strong enough to modify or transform whatever is in existence but not capable of creating it. This view is consistent with the modern scientific principles of the conservation of mass and energy. Despite this, Mimamsa philosophy refers to the Vedic teaching of life of action, which considers action as the principal constituent and rest of them as subsidiary. Thus, it can be said that Atman is considered as the agent of action and not the activity itself.

A cursory glance at Mimamsa as a school of inquiry which composes of separate schools, viz., Purva Mimamsa and Uttara Mimamsa shows that they only signify the periods to which they belong. The first school Prior Mimamsa has concentrated only on the first two parts of the Vedas. While Posterior Mimamsa has focussed its attention on the interpretations of other two- parts of the Vedas. In view of this, Purva or Prior Mimamsa thoroughly represents the activist tradition whereas the Uttara or Posterior Mimamsa is generally considered to be the end of Vedas or Vedanta.

The Materialistic Tradition

There is no denying the fact that the materialistic tradition was the first strongest reaction to the Mimamsa school. Although in view of the present day demands, the materialistic philosophy as expressed by Carvaka has been very much exaggerated, however, Carvaka never intended it to be so. Carvaka opposed tooth and nail, every branch of the Mimamsaka philosophy like epistemology, metaphysics, and even the way of life.

It is pertinent to note that the orthodox schools by and large have accepted certain sources of knowledge, such as perception, inference and verbal testimony. Although Carvaka accepted perception as the only possible valid source of knowledge, however, he has openly rejected inference and verbal testimony. One of the main criticisms levelled against the followers of this tradition is that they failed to realise properly the perception as the source of knowledge. Besides, it is difficult to say anything with certainty regarding the authenticity of the Vedas as Carvaka has openly condemned them. He also attempted to point out that Vedas cannot be relied upon owning to their self-contradictory nature. It is this theory which went against the then prevailing current of thought and still sounds to some extent sceptic or agnostic. However due to its claim for having based on the empirical knowledge or sense of perception only, it might have been able to check the premises of positivism.

In fact, quite a new picture regarding the existence of Atman painted by the Carvakas became a matter of great interest for various scholars. According to the Mimamsakas only Atman is eternal. While for Carvakas the very existence of Atman is improbable. It is beyond human capacity to perceive it. As such any attempt to prove it would be futile. It is a matter which he believed to be real for ever. There are two schools which have been continuously opposing each other, i.e., idealism and materialism. Mimamsakas were quite idealistic while Carvakas were perfectly materialistic. The gulf between them was mainly due to the different views regarding primacy of the spirit to the nature and because of conscious oppositions to materialisms by various theories developed in European philosophy. As Engels said: "The great basic question of philosophy...is that concerning the relation of thinking and being from the very early times when men, still completely ignorant of the structure of their own bodies, under the stimulus of dream apparitions came to believe that their thinking and sensation were not activities of their bodies, but of a distinct soul which inhabits the body and leaves it at death - from this time men have driven to reflect about the relation between this soul and the outside world...the answers which the philosophers gave to this question split them into two great camps. Those who asserted the primacy of spirit to nature...comprised the camp of idealism. The others, who regarded nature as primary, belong to the various schools of materialism.[25]

Thus, it can be said that Carvaka philosophy seems to have made an exclusive contribution to the philosophy of life. That is to say, it provides philosophical justification for any kind of action leading to pleasure. Moreover, he introduced a novel idea by rejecting salvation which was held in high esteem. The philosophy did not recommend the righteous path in order to achieve its objectives. This virtually discredited his philosophy and undermined its importance. Owing to this unlike the traditions of idealistic scholars, Carvaka's philosophical traditions failed to get their due status. Nevertheless, they remained an unchecked hedonistic tradition due to their enthusiasm.

The Heterodox Tradition of Jainism

It should be borne in mind that unlike the Western system the division of Indian philosophical schools into orthodox and heterodox appears quite different. The orthodox schools consider the Vedas as the main source of traditions and rely upon them in order to tackle the problem of reality. On the other hand, those schools which oppose the testimony of Vedas are called Heterodox. Although the atheistic school of thought defy the realm of spirituality and religion, however, certain heterodox traditions have emerged out of spiritual philosophies and not materialistic suppositions.

The orthodox schools consider Carvaka, Jainism and Buddhism as Nastikas, non-existence theorists. In order to understand Jainism, it is necessary to refer to early Vedic period as during that period this philosophy gained momentum due to the propagation of it by its leaders. These leaders were called Tirthankars and names of twenty four have been recorded in this regard. As far as their propoganda is concerned, they mainly relied upon the usual sources of knowledge viz., perception, inference and verbal testimony. Although these three sources were even used by the earlier schools, yet Jainas adopted a quite different approach. Unlike the Mimasakas, Jainas maintain that to know an object is to be conscious of it and it is the consciousness which is the essence of Atman. They further argued that since Atman is all pervading, it must be able to take cognizance of all objects at once. Besides, Jainism also asserts that it is the knowledge which causes transformation or modification of the consciousness of the Atman.

As far as the nature and objectives of the life are concerned, Jainism provides a new outlook. It argues that every Atman is believed to be originally pure and it is the world through which it passes. The world is pregnant with action particles, or as generally called 'Karma dust', which attack Atman and make it impure. Since it is the activity which causes degeneration of Atman and as such Jainism rightly holds the law of action responsible for this state of affairs. The action or activity which is the essence of life is considered by the Activitist traditions as the supreme God. According to Jainism, Atman loses its supreme qualities as soon as it enters in this world and consequently it is automatically bound by it.

In view of this the doctrines of even rival philosophies were preferred to find out some truth. For example, the Jainas were more keen to find out a grain of truth in any philosophy than either to outrightly reject it or approve it. In fact, it is very difficult to maintain such a position in philosophy as striking a balance between opposing schools like Idealism and Materialism well-illustrates this. Hence for Jainism, it proved to be an intellectual acrobat. Thus it can be said that Jainism also failed either to bring together the best principles of all theories or the effect any real synthesis of contradictions. At least, it could or may be considered an attempt for a superficial compromise between all the philosophical positions.

The ethical principles of the Jains were deeply noted in the theory of Karma. As H. Jacobi, who opines, points out: "The defilement of the souls takes place in the following way. Subtle matter ready to be transformed into Karma pours into the soul; this is called influx (asrava). In the usual state of things a soul harbours passions (Kasaya) which act like a viscous substance and retain the subtle matter coming into contact with the soul; the subtle matter thus caught by the soul enters, as it were, into a chemical combination with it; this is called binding (bandha) of Karma matter. The subtle matter 'bound or amalgamated by the soul is transformed into eight kinds of Karma and forms a kind of subtle body (Karmana-Sariva) which clings to the soul in all its migrations and future births and determines the individual state and lot of that particular soul."[26]

Heterodox Tradition of Buddhism

It must be borne in mind that Buddhism and Jainism resemble each other. Like Jainism, Buddhism was mainly a reform movement in India's spiritual life. It also recognised all the Gods of the orthodox tradition and denied the authority of Vedas. This is obvious from the fact that Buddhism in the beginning suspected the utility of the Vedic scriptures. As such it developed its independent doctrine which reflects the process of life. Nevertheless, it appeared that unlike Jainism, Buddhism allowed more freedom of thought to its followers. To substantiate this, it can be said that Buddhism has a number of metaphysical systems whereas Jainism has only one system.

It is necessary to note that the early texts of Buddhism were not accepted from the philosophical point of view. In fact the philosophy of Buddhism begins with Buddha. As such the Heterodox tradition of Buddhism contains gist of Buddha's teachings. Therefore, this tradition is sustained by the ethico-religious ideals as preached by Buddha himself. This theory is sometimes considered to be pessimistic as it mainly relies upon the causes of miseries in human life. However, when it depicts the revolutionary views about the universal impermanence, it gives to the extent of completely denying a permanent soul-substance. The element of suffering looms large in the four noble truths which it recommends. Besides the whole theory presents a pessimistic approach. Therefore, it is not surprising that most of the pessimistic philosophies found in Buddhism a source of inspiration. This school of thought has also influenced European philosophies. It seems that the social upheavals during that period and the strong nostalgia for the tribal life might have led Buddha to formulate such a theory. While accepting the permanence of the miseries, Buddha suggested a theory of renunciation—Nirvana in order to get rid of them. It is this aspect which brings richness and flights of this tradition. Therefore, it is necessary to examine the philosophical implications of this tradition.

Due to the simplicity of the tone, initially the followers of this tradition did not face any difficulty. However, in the period, owing to the confrontation after Buddha, by the rival schools, they had to lead their brain to revise the definitions and explanations. They had no other alternative but to transform four simple truths into doctrines. Nevertheless, the common doctrines, such as Momentariness, No Atman (denial of the existence of Atman), No God (denial of the existence of God), Relative existence and Causation were those which related to Karma.

Needless to say that the doctrine of Karma spreads large in every tradition of Indian philosophy except that of the Carvaka. The Buddhistic tradition does not believe in the Karma in order to achieve the goals of pleasure. It insists for looking beyond action to attain the Nirvana. The doctrine of momentariness speaks of only the definite stages of human life. According to this doctrine everything is momentary and subject to change. The Buddhistic tradition has elaborated this concept by considering continuity which appears but not the fact in reality. Similarly, the doctrines of No-Atman and No-God, were based on the law of momentariness as such the very existence of them was difficult to prove. However, the doctrine of relative existence shows dependency of every entity for the existence. Finally, as far as the doctrine of causation is concerned, it can be said that this doctrine has two distinct aspects, which point out that even the cause is momentary. This is because cause is aggregation and everything that we see in the world is an aggregate. Therefore, the process of aggregation decides integration while destruction of the same indicates decaying or disintegration process. Another noteworthy aspect of the doctrine of causation is that it believes that everything that comes into being is an outcome of something which departs. This is also called the doctrine of dependent origination as the effect depends on the cause.

Thus, all these doctrines if put together largely determine and explain the metaphysical position of this tradition. No doubt this tradition is laden with pessimism, nonetheless, it suggests logical remedial measures to do away with this.

The Logical Tradition of the Nyaya

It is important to note that Gautama was the founder of the logical tradition in India. Although for various reasons, there is a controversy over the period to which Gautama belonged, however, everyone acknowledges that his logical system is the most systematic.

According to this tradition, every argument must proceed with certain stipulated forms which should be logically perfect in order to avoid all possible fallacies. In view of this Salvation is considered to be the primary aim of life. This tradition considers salvation as something real and not a false hope. On account to this tradition differs from other traditions. Unlike other traditions which gave very much importance to metaphysics, Nyaya tradition attaches great importance to logic. Gautama wanted to check false philosophies as they were the outcome of sentimental debates, controversies and dialectics. A real philosophy is that which stands to the test of logic and nerges out of necessary and thereby contributes to the living traditions. It is worth noting that the two heterodox systems viz., Buddhism and Jainism, which were critical about Vedic scriptures, undergo the test of the Nyaya philosophy. Thus, Gautama's logic has been given great significance in Indian philosophy and both the orthodox and heterodox schools of thought acknowledge the validity of this logical system.

Besides, the Nyaya tradition is absolutely realistic and considers objects independent of mind and the Atman. Therefore, it considers any object of valid knowledge as real. It also believes that the very existence of the object lies beyond its scope. Hence, according to the Nyaya tradition true knowledge can be gained by the valid sources of knowledge, such as, Perception, Inference, Comparison and Verbal testimony.

The Nyaya tradition firmly believes in the doctrine of Causation. Owing to this it is not difficult to gain the knowledge about the doctrine of inference. This tradition applies its own propositions in order to understand the infrastructure of the universe. Cause is not only considered essential but given maximum importance to find out true universal propositions. It is said that besides cause-effect relationship there are certain antecedents which remain thoroughly unconditional. Therefore, cause is necessary in order to establish a condition. It is interesting to note that Nyaya tradition relies on the scientific principle which makes it to accept that space is a necessary unconditional antecedent of everything. Despite this space is not taken into consideration for determining any particular causation. Moreover, this tradition has classified cause into three kinds, i.e., the inhering cause, the non-inhering cause and the efficient cause. Nyaya also recognizes other factors of causation; such as, instrumental cause, the directive cause and the final cause. These are also known as the primary factors of causation.

Finally let us conclude this with the view expressed by Stcherbatsky: The Nyaya philosophy originated from the studies in the mythology of the public debate which was widespread in the country from considerable antiquity."[27]

The Pluralistic Tradition of the Vaisesika

Vaisesika tradition started in about 400 B.C. and has in it many aspects, such as theistic, realistic and pluralistic. In fact, Nyaya and Vaisesika differ from each other on very ordinary points. The Nyaya tradition owes its metaphysical concepts, theories to Vaisesika and in turn Vaisesika has co-ordinated its theories with the epistemological and logical theories of Nyaya. Therefore, in the traditions of Indian philosophy these two are referred at once to show their intimate relationship.

Gautama, the founder of the Nyaya tradition, emphasized sixteen categories to gain salvation. He also highlighted the need of understanding and the methods involved therein to do so. Kanada who started the Vaisesika tradition stressed on more than anything the objects of that kind of understanding as in Nyaya. Therefore, in his metaphysics we come across his categories of objects. He proposed six categories as positive and only a solitary category as negative. The group of six included substance, quality, activity, universal, particular, inherence and negation as the only negative one. The importance of the Vaisesika theory lies in its presentation of the atomic theory and the proofs for the existence of God. Most of the theories did not bother to extend their arguments beyond the plane of metaphysics. Therefore, their inquiry had more of idealism and topics of abstract nature to delve in. The scientific attitude as proposed by Vaisesika takes into account the structure of the material world, through basic elements. Although Vaisesikas recognize nine kinds of substance such as water fire, air, ether, time, space, atman, and mind, yet only five of them are considered essential. These elements constitute the material world. They are Earth, Water, Fire, Air and Ether. Out of these five elements the first four are regarded as perceivable. Certain qualities like dimension and colour are ascribed to the elements which are supposed to be perceivable. Some of the elements have only one of these qualities and even then they are accepted as perceivable elements. Vaisesikas believe that such elements have atoms bearing specific properties like smell, taste, colour and touch. Despite this, they have to be inferred as they are indivisible, indestrutible, imperceptible and also eternal. Only the evolved beings whom we call Yogis have the supernatural capacity to infer them.

One can see the basis of the atomic structure of matter explained lucidly through this school. What has been taken in the present age as the ultimate theory of atomic structure and proved with the help of complicated formulae and experiments was started long back by this tradition. However, the only possible objection could be, towards the difficult position reached by the Vaisesikas, by considering atoms as sizeless. For this the Vaisesikas have a ready argument. They presume that anything that has size is bound to be divisible and therefore, atoms should be sizeless. Another objectionable part has been the formation of a dyad due to the union of two atoms which was not perceivable to the Vaisesikas instead a triad was thought to be perceivable. The triad for them is a perceptible molecule. Similarly, time and space are viewed as two, independent, eternal, indivisible and all pervading substances. It is the time that remains as the cause of our knowledge of the past, present and future, while space is the cause of our knowledge of the directions.

Regarding the existence of God, both Nyaya and Vaisesika advance different arguments. These arguments are causal and centre round the principle of karma which is deeply rooted in the Vedic scriptures.

In brief, these causal arguments are based on the belief that there must be some cause which brings about the union of the atoms. This cause is God who is omniscient. In his absence it is impossible to make the infinitesimally small atoms to combine. The principle of karma speaks about the merits and demerits of the atmans. The qualities are in an invisible form. Creation of the world is through such Atmans which on own do not know about these hidden qualities in them. Therefore, a catalytic agent is necessary to bring out the potential of these atoms. This agent is God. The third argument is based upon the strong belief that Vedas are eternally true and authoritative. They had the authorship of God and none else. Otherwise it was impossible to have the knowledge of imperceivable infinite substances. The fourth argument considers Vedas as the source and truth and exclusively truth only. Since they advocate the existence of God there is no doubt that God exists.

The Dualistic Tradition of Sankhya

The word Sankhya means exact number or knowledge of it. This philosophy propounded by Kapila is usually viewed as atheistic and yet some of the works of Kapila may erase this because they fully subscribe to the theistic discipline. Sankhya philosophy recommends twentyfive categories. Both Jainism and Sankhya philosophy propose that atmans are many. However, unlike Jainism, Sankhya philosophy introduces material world without plurality. The word Prakriti in Sankhya philosophy implies unity among the atoms. That is why time and space have no separate existence.

The metaphysics of Sankhya philosophy is erected through an attempt to understand not only the nature of the inner being but also the external world. This is because it is pointed out that the external world keeps intimate relation with the consciousness of man. Therefore, certain questions posed by Sankhya like, how are we to follow the various forms of experience? Our understanding is supposed to be inclusive of the knowledge of the independent objective world and its connection with our consciousness. The total picture of the Sankhya metaphysics mainly revolves around Atman and Prakriti or nature. The Atman basically remains aloof but needs the assistance of Nature or Prakriti to build the material world. At the same time Nature has Reason and Reason has Ego as the components. It is under this Ego that we have four divisions like Mind, Five sensory organs, Five motor organs, and Five subtle elements. These five subtle elements join at various proportions to create five gross elements. Therefore, what we draw as the knowledge of the empirical world is from these gross elements, though their ingredients are quite different, and their source is Ego. This Ego manifests itself in the final form through Reason.

Sankhya philosophy places its arguments for being atheistic in the form of postulates and therefore, the element of denial of the commonly accepted reality of God, is very clear. The arguments commence with the validity of God as the cause or creator or the world. This is because anything that remains as cause has to change and that would contradict the God, described as perfect. A change is something inevitable as the very process of causation bears change as the condition. Similarly since God in the theistic outlook is all the while perfect, he should not be postulated even as the governor of life. Governing or controlling needs action and therefore, the controller has to be subjected to the law of change or transformation, a condition never agreeable to the theistic propositions. At the same time the very purpose of creating this world seems to be highly enigmatic. Since the theistic philosophers conceive God to be so perfect that he does not fall under the common human instincts, how could God have any desire? If he has any desire then he is no more complete or perfect in himself. Likewise, the very existence of evil which is admitted by one and all without exception sounds as defeat to the very personality of God, who is described as omnipotent, omniscient, and omnipresent. Since the description includes highly benevolent nature of God, it is a self-contradictory image of God, having permitted evil in a world which is supposed to be the result of his compassion. Lastly as the atmans are all perfect, originally and are eternal, there is no need of God to create them.

This shows that Sankhya philosophy has systematically worked out its atheism because a pure form of atheism may not accept the very existence of soul theory, God and his attributes. Therefore, Sankhya tradition has shown all the possibilities of deviation from the unchecked age-old beliefs and introduced the logic befitting the demands of atheism. It is to be accepted that Sankhya philosophy has atleast shown the limitations of the theistic model of God.

The Yoga Tradition of Patanjali

It is generally believed that the Yoga tradition of Patanjali is based upon the philosophy of Sankhya. It is also considered as a metaphysicological technique. Atman is regarded as the ultimate truth and therefore, realization of the same should be the main aim. This tradition connects the physical culture or outward reality to the inward reality because it presupposes that the roots of the outward reality are in the inward reality only. Realization of the Atman, therefore, automatically brings the seeker to know all the other forms of reality, which occupy lower positions compared to Atman.

In case of Sankhya philosophy everything that emerges from Prakriti is due to reason. In Yoga tradition it is Buddhi, the conscious which is the cause for the evolution of everything. However, both Yoga and Sankhya maintain that evolutionary process of reason and its transformation make this world. This is why we do not find much difference in the metaphysics of Sankhya and Yoga. Despite this Yoga system for its metaphysics does not require the very concept of God. Even then it does provide proofs for the existence of God. The first one is the common one, i.e., laying total trust in the Vedas or scriptures as they are infallible. The second proof is built on the basis of different rungs of power observed by us. Even by ordinary sense, one can make out that the world is full of gradations and therefore, we have ever an increasing order for the perfection of a quality. It is this view that forces us to think that the highest position might have been held by a supreme being that has infinite power, strength and knowledge. This being is God. The third proof expects some force or a special entity to unite the Atman and Nature for the sake of the creation of the world. This entity can be nothing else than God. The last proof takes advantage of the fact that every atman possesses merits and demerits. These qualities need the help of Prakriti to get displayed. Since Nature on own cannot do so, being insentient, it needs some agency to handle it, or rather guide it. Such an agency or being must be highly intelligent. None else than God can occupy this position. these essence of this system can be understood by considering reason and its transformation because it is over emphasized here that everything is due to transformation of reason. Logically, as it is stated, since everything is but a remodification of the reason, it is wise to achieve control over reason itself. Therefore, we come across the mention of the supernatural powers when control on the reason is practised. Even then a cautionary note is served by Patanjali that these practices may prove to be obstructions when the real search for salvation is made the chief aim. Instead of the word 'reason' it is better to have the usage of 'citta' because the latter as used by patanjali has five specific functions viz., Valid cognition, Invalid cognition, Ideas. Memory and sleep. The modification of Citta is a continuous process and infact control over the Citta amounts to have control over these modifications. It is interesting to find, what has been revealed by

Patanjali as impurities are infact hitches in the path of progress, i.e., Ignorance, False notion of one's ego, Desire and Attachment, Aversion, Instinctive, attachment. Further what has been suggested as the eight limbs of Yoga lead us to the final realization of the atman. They have been well expatiated in order to make every student and follower of this philosophy to understand easily the nature and forms of Yoga. These limbs serve as the guidelines to discipline one's mind and assure trans quility when honestly practised. They are self-restraint, Rules of conduct, Practice of bodily postures, control of breath, withdrawal of the senses, concentration, meditation, and samadhi or trance.

NOTES AND REFERENCES

1. Haridas Bhattacharya, The Cultural Heritage of India, p. 182.
2. A Sourcebook of Indian Philosophy, Ed. S. Radhakrishnan, pp. 27-31.
3. *Ibid.*, p. 3.
4. Aurobindo, on the Vedas, p. 5.
5. A. N. Marlow, Radha Krishnan : An Anthology, pp. 43.
6. A.C. Bose, The Call of the Vedas, p. 2.
7. A Sourcebook of Indian Philosophy, op.cit., p. 3.
8. Donald Bishop, Indian Thought, p. 38.
9. S. Radhakrishnan, Indian Philosophy, Vol. II, p. 426.
10. *Ibid.*, p. 427.
11. Louis Renou, Religions of Ancient India, p. 48.
12. D. Chattopadhyaya, Indian Philosophy : A Popular Introduction, p. 85.
13. S. Radhakrishnan, Indian Philosophy, Vol. II, p. 476.
14. A Sourcebook of Indian Philosophy, op. cit., p. 507.
15. S. Chatterjee and S. Dhirendramohan Datta, An Introduction to Indian Philosophy, p. 393.
16. *Ibid.*, p. 394.
17. William James, Pragmatism, p. 151.
18. *Ibid.*, pp. 153, 154.
19. S. Chatterjee and S. Datta, An Introduction to Indian Philosophy, op. cit., p. 412.
20. P. Nagarja Rao, Introduction to Vedanta, p. 166.
21. R. Puligandla, Fundamentals of Indian Philosophy, p. 231.
22. Donald Bishop, Indian Philosophy, p.195.
23. *Ibid.*
24. P.T. Raju, op. cit., p. 66.
25. Marx K. and Engels F., Selected Works, p. 369.
26. H. Jacobi, Sacred Books of the East, Introduction, p. 28.

3

Contemporary Indian Philosophers

The study of the chief currents of contemporary Indian Philosophy, essentially requires close examination of the influences and sources from which they emerged. This is mainly because of the notable deviations negotiated by the modern philosophers from the most resourceful ancient philosophies. It is necessary to note here that Indian traditions had been always reflective in nature and therefore, they were transformed into concrete philosophies. It was during the Vedic period that though rich literature was available, none had authored it. The interpretations still continue to pour in and they vary considerably. This indicates that the course of deviation had begun long back. Fortunately, it was the contemporary philosophers who not only devoted their works to the spirit of Indian philosophy but also tried to transevaluate it to suit the demands of the modern mind. There are several traditions which may draw our attention but in this chapter only those which have encountered the Western criticism and appeased the modern mind are selected.

This chapter examines the philosophy of Sri Aurobindo, a modern counterpart of the ancient saints and founder of an Ashram at Pondicherry; Bal Gangadhar Tilak, primarily a school teacher but destined to play the role of a political leader and then devoted to the metaphysical teaching through Gita - Rahasya; Rabindranath Tagore, a prominent leader of the nineteenth century Renaissance in the Arts; and Swami Vivekananda, a powerful advocate of the Advaita philosophy. Therefore, even in the modern period we have movements which typify in many ways like theological and practical changes occuring in

Hinduism in the nineteenth and twentieth centuries. One of the major characteristics of the modern era is the strong influence of the Western ideologies to which it has responded. Even in politics we find democratic principles at large to erect a basic philosophy. In social philosophy the demand for a Utilitarian theory, sense of justice and equality was to such a height that most of the reforms were almost organised accordingly. In academic circles introduction of western philosophies and philosophers looked inevitable. This can be confirmed in a number of books then prescribed for the philosophy curriculums of many of the Indian universities, though this had many strands. Basically Indian religions after the advent of the British, were severally criticised by the christian missionaries. This was met and corrected by the contemporary philosophical thought by providing proper reflective evaluation where the Christian critics miserably failed. However scholars like Max Muller, Paul Deussen, A.B. Keith, Dr. Annie Besant, Sir Valentine Chirol and others not only continued to study in detail the intellectual significance but also brought out similarities in the Indian and European thought. It is also true that some of the contemporary philosophers did not orient their thinking towards the Western ideology and took pride in doing so. Nevertheless, such philosophers have not disregarded the Western approach but preferred to remain loyal to the old and traditional cultural values. What is important to note in this regard is that they have done the true service by retaliating the criticism, liberating Indian thought from the western influence and reinterpreting the spirit of Indian philosophy. It is also found that most of the schools of Indian philosophy suggest a way of life and ultimate truths but unless they are made to reconcile with the contemporary thoughts, there would be no future for them in the philosophical sphere.

By and large the contemporary Indian philosophers belong to the Vedic traditions. The philosophers selected herein culled elements from different traditions for their philosophical judgements. This kind of synthesis has really reshaped the Indian thought and helped in protecting it from the customary attacks of the new materialistic and sceptical philosophical schools. Incorporating certain doctrines from the West has become a temptation and fashion of the latter half of the twentieth century. Barring a few, most of our modern philosophers could not avoid referring to the popular isms of the west. This may be because of the intention of gaining a larger platform or making the westerners understand in their own coin. Thankfully, the present situation does not force Indian philosophers to consider problems posed by western philosophers. No doubt, western philosophers are stimulated by scientific developments, positivism, and empiricism, but Indian philosophers very strictly maintain the premises of philosophy. Therefore, they do not seem to be perturbed by the developments in other fields unless that concerns philosophy as a whole.

To substantiate these views, the views of the authorities on this subject can be cited here. While expressing his dissatisfaction Radhakrishnan writes: "There is hardly any height of spiritual insight or rational philosophy attained in the world, that has not its parallel in the vast stretch that lies between the early Vedic seers and the modern Naiyayikas."[1] This was mainly because of the western attitudes towards Indian thought. Apparently this may sound a loud claim but Radhakrishnan does not necessarily mean that Indian philosophy would remain forever a source of all possible philosophical trends. At the same time contemporary Indian philosophers cannot afford to ignore the claim. In fact, each of the Indian tradition had a systematic course of development and spread over a long period to be fathomed in centuries. Therefore, this could prove to be its weakness or labile nature for not easily arriving at conclusion. Another difficulty might have been our inability to describe it in a single term or briefly define it. Philosophical traditions were generated by our own problems and inquiry. Contemporary Indian philosophers are wise in distinguishing the traditions and traditionalism. P.T. Raju observes: "The difference between the traditions of the traditionalists and philosophical traditions lies in the latter being avowedly self-respective. Otherwise even thorough-going logicalism will have to be called a type of traditionalism. Many thought forms and their impulses are rooted in our life, and aim at throwing light on the different aspects of life. Sometimes they overlap and become confused. To remove the confusions, thought generates forms of self-reflection and creates traditions of methodology, epistemology, and logic like Nyaya in India. These methodological traditions overlap other traditions, and create new problems; then philosophical thought may be pushed farther and farther from its origins."[2]

The picture at present appears to be quite different because philosophy in India has allowed itself to be influenced by the twentieth-century British Analytical Movement and specifically by the language analysis. However, as compared to the philosophy in America and England, in India it has been fairly secured since further damage is not permitted though diversity in India is in full cry. It is pointed out: "One can come across, among the younger generation of philosophers, varieties of Marxists, logical positivists, linguistic analysts, different kinds of realists and idealists and followers of several other recent western traditions."[3] In a nutshell to grasp the essence of Indian philosophy it is necessary to understand which are the values, considered as ultimate or given paramount importance. It is indeed imperative to realise that throughout the history of our-tradition there has been a uniform commitment to certain notions which signify moral perfection. Therefore, this chapter examines the philosophies of a select few who have first corrected the traditional view and then contributed to suit the modern period.

LOKMANYA BAL GANGADHAR TILAK (1856-1920)

Tilak was primarily a school teacher but was drawn to politics where he played an important role in the national movement. He was an active member of the Indian National Congress. Coming from a middle class family, he was tutored by his father in Sanskrit, Marathi and Arithmatic. Though quite involved in the freedom fight he wrote on a number of aspects of Vedas and also spread the message of self-government. His Gita Rahasya stands as one of the monumental philosophical works of the modern age. It is a work of immense value because it clarifies number of concepts, thoughts and further harmonises them. Tilak's criterion of Reality is of an exclusive view because it deviates from the past theories but at the same time tries to answer criticism levelled against Vedic suppositions. Probably due to this, Tilak's metaphysical position is looked upon as either unsteady or somewhat mystical in character. Speaking about the world he systematically approaches 'observer' and 'observed', but he directly declares our inability to determine the nature of the Absolute Reality. Therefore, his theory seems to be quite a bit agnostic in appearance though that is not the fact in reality. The usual Western or in particular the European method of analysis with regard to the world is observed in Tilak's philosophy. Herein he differentiates between the subject and the object. Tilak also holds firm belief in the ontological proof provided for the existence of the ultimate reality. He even moves a step further to consolidate his conviction through the empirical argument presented for the existence of God. Therefore, it is not a wonder that even for understanding the genuinness of the ultimate reality he recommends the Sruti texts, which are embodiment of the expressions of experiences gained by the ancient sages. For him this could ever serve as the only valid and true source for grasping the nature of the ultimate Reality. Since Tilak has picked up every fibre of the spirit of Gita and also Upanishads, he asks: "In what way those theories can be scientifically supported."[4]

Tilak feels that the Upanishadas, the Brahmasutras, and the Gita are the bedrock of the Vedic religion. They have constituted Vedic religion through some of the common principles. That is why Vedic religion enjoys the seat of authority almost in an eternal fashion. The two paths which have taken such a lead in the philosophical race are Renunciation and Energism. In fact the principles in support of these two paths have been pleaded by the Upanishads while they are given a shape in the Brahma-Sutra. In the Gita, though directly the path of renunciation is not pushed forward it is observed that the spirit is channelised through the theme such that it ends up by propounding a basic detachment towards everything. However, at no rate Karma Yoga theoretically supplements the concept. It first lays emphasis on work and hopes to evaporate the subsequent expectations by way of building up detachment towards rewards. Therefore, the concept of Karma Yoga has really opened more vistas for the Vedic religion.

Concept of Dharma

The term 'Dharma' often appears in the different schools of Indian religious philosophy. Without clarifying the concept of one's own Dharma, it is difficult to claim any status. Dharma literally means 'righteous thinking', 'right path', or 'right action'. Much owing to the variety of meanings drawn from the word, every philosopher who is concerned about the righteous path in life interprets something new as it appeals to him. Tilak is no exception to this. However, when it comes to the explanation of an 'ism', the philosopher often relies upon his fundamental convictions that result out of his idea of 'Dharma'. The term has been encompassing larger sectors in the field of philosophy and therefore, it is becoming quite complex. Formerly it was a practice to restrict it to religions and religious philosophies. Due to the development of 'moral philosophy', which partly proved to be an offshoot of religions it became necessary to treat the problem of right action just as the problem of evil as of fundamental importance. However, even before the western philosophers who were trying to build up philosophies Indian philosophers were engaged with such problems. Therefore, it is no wonder that even in the epics the problem of right action is attended to. In attempting the problems of moral philosophy, philosophers from East the West alike, tried to ascribe various meanings and also postulated theories.

At the very outset, Tilak begins by stating that it is not very proper to just translate the term 'Dharma' into a simplified or equivalent form to suit one's own concept. This is because, for him, 'Dharma' by itself is a complex term. It cannot be erected satisfactorily by providing only meanings. It has many sheaths which have to be peeled off before describing it correctly. Apart from the fact that the term can vary with every individual, it has also global applications owing to which it may stand as something highly impersonal. In its very fundamental form it has been defined as 'respectable behaviour'; in terms of its origin as custom; and as limitations or restrictions imposed for the welfare of the society.[5] In spite of these recognised definitions Tilak thinks that such definitions are inadequate because they are ever liable to change due to the demand of the changing situations and onslaught of modernity. The other argument normally presented by the propounders of the theory of right action is based upon empirical judgement. This is the most easy and common way of proving the basic tenets of a philosophy. According to this it is always safe to refer to the precepts of the sages who are the enlightened personalities. Their experiences are too invaluable and therefore, the path followed by the venerable personalities should be taken up as standard. Tilak feels that this cannot be the ultimate and that too a faultless solution because, even sages differ in their interpretations and this would force us to examine the right sense of the term 'venerable' as applied to the evolved beings. On this basis, Tilak thinks"... venerable persons cannot mean a large collection of men, since following a large collection of ignorant men is like the blind following the blind. It cannot mean 'learned men' as there is no conformity or uniformity in their action."[6]

It shows that Tilak is eager to discover the Dharma based on universal principles, which can remain tenable in all possible circumstances. As he is more concerned about the consistency of the theory of Dharma, to be proposed, he seems to be quite rigid regarding the right sense, right implication and right-application of Dharma. Time being one such powerful factor, always bears the capacity to alter things in proportion to itself. Therefore, Tilak is highly practical in eliciting the truth which majority of the philosophers have successfully avoided. Another aspect which Tilak wants to expatiate is through the metaphysical view taking care of time and person together. That is why he does not agree with the common theory of good and evil demanding"... rather to the men of intuitive moral genius-to the prophets and the sages - that we should go for advice as to the ultimate purpose and meaning of life."[7]

This is what prompts Tilak to refute the age-old views of the materialistic and theological schools. He calls them 'extreme and imperfect views". These views separately try to explain the theory of right action but in doing so they do not allow the possibility of inter-connection on certain issues, beliefs and principles within themselves. Had it been done, a much more workable and agreeable theory could have come forward. Therefore, both the materialistic view of happiness and the intuitional view of the theological outlook, cannot satisfactorily explain the theory of Dharma. Tilak expects the metaphysical view to do the necessary corrections and present the right interpretation. It is at this stage that we understand how Tilak clearly maintains his position totally different from the Western philosophers. The usual elaborative descriptions provided by the western philosophers about materialism, intuitionism and metaphysics do not tally with the concepts developed by Tilak. For Tilak even the western metaphysical view is very close to the materialistic view. In Indian philosophy, metaphysical view is called Adhyatmika which covers up a wide range that includes even spiritual aspects. Therefore, the metaphysical view as proposed by Tilak covers up the influence of the force or factor which motivates the external world. This force that exists in the human body is referred by Tilak as consciousness or more appropriately *Cittasakti*. It is responsible to relate human soul 'atman' to the universe. At a later stage Tilak connects action and happiness. Although many a time Tilak and Immanuel Kant are compared on this issue, they have clearly maintained certain viewpoints in opposition. Basically,

Kant has supported the moral argument with an intention to adjust this world morally. It looks highly idealistic. The basic principle that underlies the argument takes advantage of the fact that if moral values have to be sanctioned an objective existence in the world, the world must be morally adjusted. If this is not granted then the very functioning of the infinite mind (God) would be impossible and the moral order will have no stand. Thus attributing a moral order is compulsory in view of the exhibition of the objectivity of the moral laws. Tilak argues in a different way. He presumes that every action is an opposition to unhappiness or in pursuit of happiness. Happiness by itself has categories. They include the utilitarian view, enlightened a self-interest, purely self-centered, and selfishness. It is in fact difficult to differentiate between the third and fourth categories. Tilak is of the opinion that it is the intensity of happiness that decides the category. In broad division the selfish and the utilitarian fall apart as rival viewpoints. The only form of happiness which is sought after due to the enlightened self-interest may escape any criticism but the rest according to Tilak are not through in their approach. Therefore, they are likely to remain always imperfect. If the utilitarian theory concentrates only on the quantitative aspect, then it would be handicapped easily. Unless it enjoins the qualitative aspect, nothing worthwhile is possible. Therefore, even the materialistic theory of happiness has failed to explain 'in what lies the happiness of people' the method of ascertaining it and 'by whom it has to be ascertained."[8] Tilak feels that in this theory of happiness the motivation, reason, moral order and will are ignored. This is how Tilak tries to show that the shade of difference between selfishness and selflessness is only apparent. He wants to banish this apparent conflict with an intention to bring together all the virtuous qualities under 'humanness' to serve as a preface to the required moral order. Therefore, any act which tries to enrich the moral order is a virtuous one while anything that denigrates it is a vice. This could only remain as a test for befitting as a quality in the true sense.

Tilak also analyses the impulses delivered by intuition, but in a different way. At first he detests the idea that all impulses are genuine. For him the genuineness of an impulse depends upon the source which supplies it. It is the conscience residing in the mind, which truly guides us to discriminate between good and bad. Although this would seem to be an old concept Tilak cautions us by declaring that everything that is impelled by this conscience may not necessarily be the dictates of conscience. The main truth which can interrupt this process is the limitations of our mind and also its nature. Since in the Indian philosophy certain divisions with regard to the nature of the mind is suggested, Tilak presumes that only the one either constituted or disciplined by the spiritual values can have the capacity to discriminate. The different natures viz., Sattvika, Rajasa and Tamasa show the gradation in the descending order. The first one is the only one as already described, to be relied upon. The second one with its limited capacity is extremely feeble and therefore, cannot be totally trusted. The third one is notably irreliable because although devoid of the desirous qualities it may even mislead. Of course, Tilak has reinterpreted the verses of Gita, however, while doing this he has clarified what kind of intuition is to be valued and how to judge the pure reason and its implications. Tilak has provided certain confirmatory tests to judge the substance that constitutes the intuition. The Sattvika type of mind as recommended by him always accommodates pure reason so that it can execute the bodily organs for the corresponding actions. Yet another sign of this mind is the happiness derived out of such Sattva and therefore, it is called Sattvika metaphysical happiness. The other types have sense contact and inertia or sleep as basic needs to generate happiness. A person having such minds can never content self and therefore, will be full of negative qualities. He cannot be free from antinomies. Thus, Tilak says: "The foundation of ethics is the frame of mind and mode of life of a self-realised person".[9]

Tilak and Kant

It is necessary to understand and mention in brief Kant's philosophy, particularly his ethical stand point. Kant believed that when we say something as ought to be or ought not to be are issuing a command or imperative. Therefore, one of the ways of formulating a moral requirement is always through an imperative. Thus, judgements about what we should or should not do are best understood by classifying them as imperatives. According to Kant, the imperatives are of two kinds. The first one, hypothetical imperative which provides knowledge for achieving what is desired. Therefore, attaining the purpose could be through a hypothetical imperative. However, Kant does not believe that the imperatives of morality are hypothetical. It is on this basis that Kant holds fast to his moral argument to show the strength of his ethical standpoint. He says: "In a situation of moral choice, what you should do does not depend upon what you want or upon what is convenient to you."[10] As such Kant recommends the second type of imperative which is categorical imperative and unconditional. He too asserts that moral imperatives are categorical, rather a straight-forward command that directs the path. Thus, it becomes obvious as to why like Tilak, Kant totally rejects the utilitarian outlook. He refutes the loud claims of utilitarianism because to him an ethics whose goal is the pleasure of human beings cannot be based upon categorical imperatives. At best, it yields to the form of hypothetical imperatives. He says: "If you want to become happy, or if you want others to become happy, then you should do such... the notion of happiness is so indefinite that although every man wishes to attain it, yet he never can say definitely and consistently what it is that he really wishes and wills."[11] An ethic of happiness, says Kant, does not provide clear-cut principles of conduct. "We cannot therefore, act on any definite principle to secure happiness, but only an empirical counsels, for example, of regimen, frugality, courtesy, reserve, etc., which experience teaches do, on the average, most promote well being... The problem to determine certainly and universally what action would promote the happiness of a rational being is completely insoluble."[12]

Kant not only depicts the premises of morality on the basis of its imperative characteristics but also gives a clue to understand its validity. He points out that if morality consists of categorical imperatives, how can one know when he is failed with a genuine and binding categorical imperative? In other words he desires to provide a test for checking its validity. Kant proposes universality as the test of moral obligation. In this regard, he thinks that every person's reasoning as an outcome of maxim of the action. He contends that to test a maxim one should ask what it would be like if, people in general were to act upon it. Again Kant argues that if maxims were universalized a kind of contradiction would occur. Therefore, the test for determining which maxims are permissible as valid principles of action is formulated by Kant in his famous categorical imperative. "Act only on that maxim whereby thou canst at the same time will that it should become a universal law."[13] This is called the uni versalization test. However, Kant remarks that some of the maxims involve in a kind of contradiction or conflict when universalized and as a result of it they represent wrong conduct. Therefore, morally permissible actions should be totally free from conflicts and contradictions. When Tilak's philosophy is gauged through Kantian angle, it seems that somehow the streams of their ethical thought run parallel. The ethical philosophy of both these philosophers is based on the presumption of the duality extant in the nature of man. The double nature of man consists of irrational and rational parts. Both consider Reason superior. This leads them to believe that morality consists in being rational or being free from appearances. The supreme moral law is the law of reason and is determined a priori, because 'a philosophy which mixes up pure principles with empirical ones, does not deserve the name of philosophy."[14] Goodness or badness of an act depends entirely on the quality of will and not on consequences. Man is free to do what his reason dictates. Both think that though man is phenomenally bound he is noumenally free.

Besides, both Kant and Tilak make a distinction between reason and will, while preparing the ground work of the metaphysic of morals. Kant makes it clear by stating that the private purpose of man must be subordinated to reason because it is the reason that governs the will. This means that Kant like Tilak stresses upon the universalization of reason than on the inclinations. While comparing the moral philosophy of Tilak and Kant, with regard to the moral philosophy, it may be pointed out that as in Kant the senses are treated as subordinate and it is the whole aim of moral philosophy to teach a law which helps the Atman to be free from the fetters of senses.[15] Therefore, it may be safely added that the moral law given by Kant and Tilak dis parages that section of human nature which is ruled by inclinations while it extols the one managed by reason. The emergence of inclination, according Tilak in particular, may be for a variety of reasons and so its pattern cannot be declared as uniform throughout. However, Kant clarifies what he means by the moral law and its implications. The motives and content of moral action in Kant is duty. When an act is performed for no other reason than it should be done, the content and the motive unify significantly. Therefore, Kant thinks that likewise only that action has moral worth which is performed 'not from inclination' but from the sense duty. Green has pointed out"... that acting according to the laws pre-supposes a consciousness of ends to be attained in conformity with those laws. This end is absent in Kant where both the content and the motive of an action are duty. This formalism is corrected in Tilak where the motive is duty no doubt, but the content is merely duty. We are called upon to make our Buddhi Sama and discharge disinterestedly the duty of liberation of others."[16] Here we have plain proof that drawing of the moral good with mere beneficient social activities cannot be a perfect moral experience. It cannot be a right assessment to show one of these two great thinkers, in comparison, has not reached the peak in the metaphysical position. It is a general tendency to overestimate one thinker and underestimate the contemporaries. No doubt, Tilak and Kant may be compared to found a new identification. In fact at best, Tilak and Kant may be compared to show certain similarities in their outlooks but a complete discrimination would prove unwise. This is because, unlike Tilak, Kant did not rely on any scriptures and their interpretations. Kant's moral argument in philosophy begins with furnishing of proofs for the existence of God and then deciding a moral order for the world and self. He has also hit at something fundamental in devising his universalization test. This automatically involves a basic aspect of our conduct towards others. Even then, it may be pointed out that universalization fails as a sole test and this could be a subject for the criticism of Kant's ethics. In Vedantasara Hiriyanna comments,"... one moral point from the Advaita metaphysics of Tilak and in this he rises superior to Kant. Tilak ascribes only one end to an individual both in his own case and in the case of others. An individual has to strive for his own liberation and also try for the liberation or perfection of others. According to Tilak, a Sthitaprajna will not strive only for the worldy good but for the spiritual good of mankind. Thus he aims at the spiritual upliftment of all, which is Sarvamukti."[17]

Tilak's Views on Happiness and Unhappiness

As far as the scope of happiness in life is concerned, there is a great deal of difference between the Eastern and Western philosophers. It is held that the good life is also the intelligent life and the freedom of man from the old traditions lead him to behave on the basis of a distinct philosophy. In life, while re-stating certain principles, Tilak points out the necessity of a living philosophy. Apart from the usual criteria suggested by the

Eastern and Western philosophers, Tilak suggests the criterion of actability as the true philosophic test. He observes: "Our philosophers have accepted the position that every human being in this world is continually struggling in order to obtain happiness, or to increase the amount of happiness which he has obtained, or to obviate or reduce his unhappiness."[18] This cannot be regarded as a kind of philosophical judgement since it appears to be an observation based on experience. Nevertheless, there is no denying the fact that man can achieve happiness, if unhappiness is prevented.

The doctrine that pleasure or happiness is the chief good in life is known as hedonism. Even since the time of Jeremy Bentham and John Stuart Mill in the nineteenth century, utilitarianism has been considered as based on the hedonistic doctrine. This doctrine describes pleasure as the major aim in life assuming thereby a number of forms like Psychological hedonism, Egoistic hedonism and Altruistic hedonism. It is the ethical and altruistic forms of hedonism that are found to be inherent in Tilak's philosophy of happiness. He says that it is wrong to presume that man always seeks to gain pleasure and avoids pain though in fact he ought to do so. Probably, he preferred to uphold Altruistic view in order to serve the interests of the majority. While referring to the ancient schools of Indian philosophy, Tilak disagrees with the customary explanation which subjects happiness to the whims of the deities. He asserts that the causes of those two should be sought at the physical or metaphysical levels. In this connection, the Vedantic classification as 'adhidaivika (God given)', 'adhibhautika (physical)', and 'adhyatmika (metaphysical)' with regard to the source of happiness or unhappiness serves the purpose. Nevertheless, Tilak does not rely upon the proofs of any philosophy because he is aware of the fact that these have been moulded due to the hold of religious scriptures. According to him what we need today is very apparent and does not correspond to the five primordial elements. He says: "Whether we look upon pain and happiness as of two kinds or three kinds, nobody wants pain; therefore, it is stated both in the Vedanta and the Samkhya philosophies that preventing every kind of pain to the greatest possible extent and obtaining the uttermost and the permanent happiness is the highest goal of man."[19] This view also resembles with what J.S. Mill says:"... the creed which accepts as the foundation of morals, utility, or the greatest happiness principle, holds that actions are right in proportion as they tend to promote happiness, wrong as they tend to produce the reverse of happiness. By happiness is intended pleasure and the absence of pain; by unhappiness, pain and the privation of pleasure."[20] Tilak appears to be not at all satisfied with this analysis and therefore, he attempts to examine what has been termed as the uttermost, the real, and the permanent happiness. Likewise he expects the solutions to the problems like whether such happiness can ever be attained? Whether pain and happiness are two independent or different kinds of sufferings, experiences? And whether the absence of one can be referred to as the other on the principle that 'that which is not light, is darkness'.[21] Ultimately Tilak relies upon what has been acknowledged in Bhagwatgita. He has exerted to show that the doctrine does not recommend a total abandonment of Action to obviate evil effects. Tilak opines that the dictum of Samnyasa school, that all happiness arises from the prevention of pain cannot be accepted as completely perfect. Further he adds that when one voluntarily wants to re-experience a thing it is a desire and when the desire becomes strong it is transformed into thirst. To conclude he suggests that material happiness is by its nature, wholly dependent on the organs, irrespective of the result of our doing so.

Thus, Tilak attempts to point out that pain and happiness are two independent and different sufferings. It is impossible to satisfy all our desires in order to gain happiness. The theory of Karma lays down that the most meritorious thing to do is not to completely destroy our thirst but continue to perform all actions without expecting any fruit. Tilak opines that the genre of philosophical standpoint here demands the accepting of the fact that the happiness of enjoying objects of pleasure, is in itself a happiness of enjoying objects of pleasure, is in itself a happiness. However it is always insufficient, inconstant and inhuman. Therefore, the true ideal of man who adores reason must be higher than such a type of happiness. While adhering to this principle Tilak relates true ideal to self-realization. In this context, the true ideal is the happiness of the peace and Tilak insists that this is possible only if the metaphysical happiness is treated to some extent superior to the material happiness. In this regard Tilak deviates from the philosophy of renunciation which tries to maintain purely metaphysical plain and disdains anything other than it. Tilak often describes the metaphysical happiness by equating it to peace or emancipation. He takes a clue from what has been already explained in detail in Gita regarding the qualities of a Sthitaprajna. He is a person who has realisation and remains highly content with himself. Having identified self for him there are no antinomies to mar his cheerfulness. Doing the duty with no attachment, he maintains the equable frame of mind throughout. Thus Tilak insists that the foundation of ethics, is the frame of mind and mode of life of a self-realised person.[22] Thus, man has to make a choice to elect out of the two existing forms of happiness i.e., the transient external pleasure of the organs which is common while the other one is true and leads to permanent benefit. The second is very difficult to obtain. However, a wise man always prefers latter because of its intensive characteristics. It is through reason that the internal or metaphysical happiness can be obtained. The materialistic happiness is very transient. Materialism cannot satisfactorily explain the reason i.e., why moral principles have permanence which does not depend upon the external conditions. Tilak observers : "For, whatever general doctrine is laid down by reference to happiness in the external world, yet in as much as all happiness or unhappiness or unhappiness is inherently transient, all doctrines of morality founded on such a transient foundation are equally weak, i.e., non-permanent; and, on that account, the everlasting permanence of the law of truth seen in one's being ready to sacrifice one's life in the interests of truth, irrespective of considerations of happiness or unhappiness, cannot be based on the doctrine of the 'greatest happiness of the greatest number."[23] Tilak's arguments regarding happiness are based on the philosophy of Gita though while explaining them in detail he cites both eastern and western concepts. Hence, very often, we come across the references of behavioural doctrines which never had any influence on the scriptures.

The Moral Law as a Practical Guide

Tilak's concept of Dharma is based on the moral law and that justifies the principles of morality as the supreme principle. He holds that the moral law can be discussed and put into practice since it is potent enough to function as a categorical imperative. Evenness of mind - Samyabudhi - is the chief component of morality and as such it has to be imbibed. Tilak believes that the formulation of this law provides guidelines for practical life.

However, he opines that despite our freedom of actions we are bound by Atman and therefore, all our actions must be consistent with it. Tilak asserts: "The knowledge of the unity of Brahman and Atman is the basis of both theory and practice."[24] Therefore, what is needed is to find out how does the evenness of mind serve as a practical guide and lay down the foundation of morality in practice?

The philosophy of Gita as presented by Tilak has to be related to the attainment of equanimity with beneficient consequences. Nevertheless, this may lead to the medicore analysis of the essence of practical life and may not allow anything to be philosophical in concrete terms. Hence while referring this point, Tilak says that the actions need not be performed for the sake of the consequences. The moment one becomes conscious of the intention of the actions like selfless or altruistic, the very purpose is defeated. Usually, no sooner does the pride enter while performing an action then the humility automatically departs. Thus, the presence of pride and absence of humility adversely affect the spirit and qualify of actions. Tilak insists upon the suggestion made by Bhagwatgita i.e., one must endure to strive upon the path of disinterested action or Niskama Karma. Even Sankara's commentary on this subject resembles Tilak's interpretation though Tilak has drawn his theory from the philosophy of Gita for the modern times. "Actions become bereft of their natural tendency of binding when done with equanimity."[25] While describing Niskama Karma, Tilak synonymously uses the terms Yogi and Karmayogi. Very often, 'Niskama Karma' is misunderstood as something which negates action. This is because the whole stress is laid upon detaching self from the consequences. If this sort of judgement is upheld then it is necessary to clarify that despite this anticipation, offering of all actions to God is the positive aspect of it and certainly a unique one. "The Gita" says, D.S. Sarma, "is not a cold gospel of duty for duty's sake. It is gospel of duty for God's sake."[26] Therefore, what might appear a sort of oxymoron with reference to Niskama Karma has to be judged carefully. What is suggested is that at any stage one should not give up the actions but perform them without expecting any fruit.

Tilak anticipates certain obstacles in the way of putting the supreme moral principle into practice. The usual actions whose consequences are injurious may challenge such principles. It is the consequences which matter most otherwise one may not bother to ratify the actions. Under such circumstances the validity of the moral law will certainly be questionable. Tilak points out that the moral law affirms the worth of an action taking into consideration the purity of the motive of the doer. In fact, Tilak is confident that actions which lead to immoral consequences are not performed by those who seek the realisation of God. Besides, patriotism, responsibilities, family and personal or impersonal loyalties etc., may lead a man to perform actions which are morally not justifiable. They give rise to narrow views and differences of mine and thine and thereby conflict with the much adored Samyaboudhi- equanimity of mind. Tilak flouts the objection by pointing out that these limited virtues are stages by which a man's intellect may attain to Samatva.[27] A long as a comprehensive ideal is not achieved one's own interests have to be sacrificed. The loyalty to a limited interest is to be subsumed under loyalty to a wider interest. It is in this way the realisation of God should be achieved.

It can be seen that Tilak does not elongate his philosophy so that it goes beyond the limits of rationality. Having considered reason as the most important species in his theory, he disallows sentiments to supercede it. According to Tilak Samayabuddhi does not ask us to forgive a criminal when we know that he is an enemy of the society.[28] What is needed is that through Samatva punishment should not be inflicted for a personal end. In case of conflicts of opinion, one should stick up to the standards of the absolute moral law. Thus, it can be said that this philosophy is not something as unworldly or impracticable. Nevertheless, the problem which crops up in this connection is that whether an individual who abides by the standards of moral law can be guaranteed of satisfaction? In fact, this is a persistent problem and it is difficult to find out a permanent solution on it. Those who practise the moral law usually descend to the world of common men and attain bliss.

Although, no doubt there are number of idealistic views which coincide with the spirit of the moral law, however, the controversy between contemplative life and active life continues. Referring to Plato and Aristotle, Tilak points out: "The highest aim of life according to Plato is the vision of the Sun of Reality or the contemplation on the idea of the good. This life in spirit is something in which a philosopher would merge himself and would not like to come out. Aristotle's God is the thinking theoria and his happiness lies in eternal self-contemplation. Both Plato and Aristotle sing the glories of contemplative life; but they do not forget man's duties towards society...... And Aristotle includes practical wisdom in his conception of the wise man. Thus a man who has attained to Jnana owes a great duty to society."[29] Thus it can be said that Sankara and Tilak advocate principle of partial renunciation of our acts which imply that work is not the object of renunciation but the positive consequence of it, i.e., fruit which is the object of renunciation. In short, their theory is the theory of a fruit renunciation.

We are well familiar with the efforts made by different philosophers to bring about reconciliation between thesis and antithesis although an antinomy exists. A similar antinomy between renunciation of work and continuation of work can be reconciled.But this would need sufficient time to work. Tilak provides different meanings to the word Jnana i.e., illumination or experience of reality. Nevertheless, usually it is used in the sense of knowledge which does not cover the theory of Jivanmukta. Therefore, "Jnana is not to be understood as an event but a process says Professor Ranade, "this process is almost never ending. It is similar to the process of meeting of the curve and the base line of a hyperbola. One approaches the end but very gradually and one may not find the goal in hand. Thus the individual is traversing the path of knowledge or is making an asymptotic approximation to it."[30] In this regard, the difficulty which arises is that how to ascertain that an individual has acquired the stage of absolute or still struggling for it? Tilak holds that a Jivanmukta need not be considered a totally liberated individual but the one who has been at the advanced level. That is to say he emphasises on the percentage of achievement.Thus, he does not consider a Jivanmukta a perfect being like a Siddha personality. Therefore, the former should continue to act and allow himself to be influenced by the actions which are performed. Even after illumination one has to be actively involved.

Tilak has been subjected to criticism on the ground that his metaphysics and activistic ethics do not go together and also lack logic. On the other hand Sankara's philosophy is considered more consistent with Advaitism and Quietism. However, it is true that Tilak does not accept the contention that Advaitism should necessarily be coupled with Karma-Sanyasa. He believes that Sankara's doctine is two-fold. First, it has Absolutism along with the theory of illusion and secondly it advocates renunciation of all activism. Tilak opines that these two aspects cannot be logically connected and an attempt to do so may result into an inconsistent and self- contradictory theory. According to him it is wrong to say that the basic presumption of the Advaita philosophy and that of the theory of Renunciation are similar. At best they may be recognised as co-existing entities, nevertheless, they cannot be related. In fact, these theories cannot be followed without activity and renunciation should not be considered as giving up of the activities. Anyone who gains the knowledge of equanimity, for him moral actions automatically become sort of a primary commandment. In the words of Spinoza: "He would be doing good but will all the while be unaware that he is doing good because an action is done by him not because he chooses it as good but because it is the natural consequences of his character."[31] Similarly Abott says:"A being which gave itself the moral law, and whose, freedom, therefore, is Autonomy, would not be conscious of obligation or duty, since the moral law would coincide with its will."[32]

It can be said that the moral behaviour is a natural consequence. The only point worth noting here is that the Jivanmukta cannot liberate himself from the earthliness and like others, he has to continue for his sense of equanimity which makes him quite unique. The exclusive positive aspect of the Jivanmukta is his general disinterestedness, owing to which evil activities remain far away from him. This is also because he is more concerned with the Divine plane though involved in the physical plane which he cannot totally avoid. While expressing his views on imperatives,Kant upholds Tilak's point of view. According to him the imperative has no meaning when applied to the Divine will or other Holy will; it is surely limited to those beings whose will is imperfect. Lastly, it can be said that the philosophical commandment proposed by Tilak aims at the perfection of oneself with the intention of perfecting others. Thus, it includes both in the process of perfection.

RABINDRANATH TAGORE (1861-1941)

It is exceedingly difficult to appraise the genius of a philosopher who is also an eminent poet. Much owing to a different kind of metaphysical standpoint held by the poet-philosopher, a student of philosophy is faced with own limitations. Therefore, apprehending such a thinker is a challenging task. Since Rabindranath Tagore relied totally on the vision, in its true spiritual meaning, he did not allow the kind of logic and the dialectical method usually preferred by philosophers to establish a new tradition. It should also be remembered that every philosophy emerges out of the social or the personal demands of the philosopher's nature and that is why it has to strafe the non-philosophical tendencies right at the inception. In case of Tagore, being a visionary, truth is revealed to him through the poetic images. A spark of mysticism kindles untiringly and therefore, nothing seems to be deliberately philosophical. It is and shall ever remain the demand of the (mystic) philosophy to detect the truth only after passing beyond the poetic images because a poet-philosopher has a unique world to gather realisation. In Tagore's own words, "If you shut your door to all errors, truth will be shut out."[33] The feelings, urges and realisations for Tagore required a powerful index of philosophical inquiries.

Broadly speaking Indian philosophy had been concentrating on two main facets i.e., one of them serving the purpose of materialism and the other holding on to spiritualism. The conflict between these two schools was minimised from time to time, stating that both are the shades of the same Reality. Despite this, it seemed impossible to bridge the gap. One of the reasons could be that the school of materialism and its supporters were keen on affirming worldly values while rest had a pursuit for spiritual values. However, the Upanisads affirm both the personal God and the impersonal Absolute. They propose both life-affirmation and life-negation. Sankara's advaita attributes final reality to Brahman and therefore, anything other than Brahman is deplorable. Vaisnava sects insist that the personal God and the world together constitute the ultimate reality. Tagore's writings are deeply influenced by the teachings of the Upanisads. Some of the poems reflect the Upanisadic wisdom. In the preface to 'Sadhana', Tagore admits: "The writer has been brought up in a family where texts of the Upanisads are used in daily worship; and he has had before him the example of his father who lived his long life in the closest communion with God while not neglecting his duties to the world or allowing his keen interest in all human affairs to suffer any abatement." He also observes: "To me the verses of the Upanisads and the teachings of Buddha have ever been things of the spirit and therefore, endowed with boundless vital growth."[34]

What appeals Tagore maximum is considering God as personal and adorable. His methodology is to check the philosophical current which leads to the realization of God. In case it is strapped by the feeling of love then only it is worthy for Tagore to propose as a true philosophy. Therefore, he emphasizes the relation of love between man and God. Therefore, in Gitanjali he approves the world and life affirmation as -

> "Deliverance is not for me in renunciation. I feel the embrace of freedom in a thousand bonds of delight. Thou ever pourest for me the fresh draught of thy wine of various colours and fragrance, filling this earthen vessel to the brain. My world will light its hundred different lamps with thy flame, and place them before the altar of thy temple. No, I will never shut the doors of my senses. The delights of sight and hearing and touch will bear thy delight. Yes, all my illusions will turn into the illumination of Joy, and all my desires ripen into fruits of love."[35]

It is at this stage that one can understand the thorough influence of Vaisnavism though a certain margin is to be reserved to show Tagore's genius in pruning certain isms, before arriving at a new platform. Vaisnavism does not dismiss the world as illusion. The world, for a Vaisnava is as real as the individuals living in it. For him the personality of God is complete only if these two are identified as real. It is observed that usually while expressing reverence for the ultimate the other realities are viewed as subsidiaries. It is in this context, that Tagore brings out what he imagines as God with qualities. According to him realization of God is possible only through love and nothing else. The love ought to be pure love. In this regard he differs from the Vaisnavism because the latter expects God - realization only in a supernatural order of existence. Love as popularly thought is not the concept recommended by Tagore. Love as popularly thought is not the concept recommended by Tagore. He wants its expression through the universal language, like sound, touch and colour. He also feels that man need not look for salvation anywhere else, but can definitely achieve it on the earth itself.

In Indian philosophy, the world 'Darsana' has a special meaning and therefore, simply translating it as 'vision' would be incorrect. In terms of the philosophical wisdom, it is 'vision of the real'. What has been usually felt is that Tagore conveys much of his philosophy through his poems is very true. This is because for a poet philosopher, the medium is ever his verse and philosophy automatically flows. In 'Religion of Man' he says, "I have already made the confession that my religion is poet's religion. All that I feel about it is from vision and not from knowledge. Frankly, I acknowledge that I cannot satisfactorily answer any question about evil or about what happens after death. Nevertheless I am sure that there have some moments in my own experience when my soul has touched the infinite and has become infinitely conscious of it through the illumination of joy."[36] This indicates that Tagore did not believe in nor ever tried the conventional methods for searching the meaning of Reality. The usual logical methods which are considered very essential for analysis, were never handled by Tagore. It shows the perspicuity observed in his language is a proof of his reading of the "Vision", but not reflection of a particular school of thought. Being a natural philosopher he comments, "The meaning of the living words that come out of the experiences of great hearts can never be exhausted by any one system of logical interpretation."[37] However, when a student of philosophy tries to note the novelty of his philosophy, he does come across a number of isms but at no point his philosophy looks being strapped. Although, with the accepted norms of the academic philosophy Tagore's philosophy has to be studied yet there seems to be a strongly guided surrealistic element in his poetry. It may be because of the early impressions carried by his mind were mostly the ancient Indian ideals. He also felt an urge for the tenets of the Vaisnavism combined with the ardour for the Bhakti-Yoga. That is why we find a rare synthesis of philosophy, religion and lyrical outburst.

We have a number of opinions from different schools on Tagore's philosophy. Hirendra Datta calls it the philosophy of concrete Monism. [38] It is because of Tagore's insistence on conceiving reality in the true monistic fashion, that is, it is concrete and one. This may also be because the Monism which remains concrete can embrace a number of realities and does not negate other realities. This means Tagore's Reality can accommodate all realities or is the ultimate reality. Radhakrishnan says, "We do not know whether it is Rabindranath's own heart or the heart of India that is beating here."[39] This may sound as a personal fascination towards Tagore's merits but since Tagore's philosophy is designed in a natural form and to suit the demands of the modern times, such an analysis must have arrived out of a perfect apprehension. Therefore, with all his poetic insight and high idealism, he is an idealist as well as a spiritualist, a monist as well as a theist.

Tagore's Idealism

Tagore's idealism is not restricted to a typically erected metaphysical world just because it emerges out of poetic insight but it is down to earth. His strong humanistic beliefs have created a world in which a perfect theistic humanism resides. What is important for Tagore is the strong bond that ties Humanity and Divinity. Ancient philosophies of India have maintained a gulf between these two and though the passage is suggested, it expects much of the exertion only from Humanity. For Tagore this is not an acceptable proposition. He expects divinity in man and humanity in God. He thinks that man is, at times, elevated to the status of God, while God is discovered sometimes in man. This means that divinity can descend to the human level or humanity may reach the Divine. Unless these two make a way for themselves into the grounds of each other it is impossible for Tagore's idealism to go for completion. Tagore also believes that unless everything is understood and interpreted in the human way joy cannot be derived. In 'Religion of Man' he describes: "The idea of the humanity of our God, or the divinity of man, the eternal, is the main subject of this book."[40] Tagore also tries to establish a personal touch between man and objects. One may draw the impression that he attempts to handle two widely differing philosophical attitudes, viz., the empirical and the esoteric. It is in this light that he imagines that an intellectual approach to Nature and to the problems of life can truly make a dispassionate survey. While judging Rabindranath Tagore as a philosopher, V.S. Narvane writes: "Poets are not always amiably disposed towards philosophers. Keats complains that philosophy can clip an angel's wings' and that all charms fly at the cold touch of philosophy. In another passage, Keats seems to suggest that the philosopher and the poet are 'sheer opposites' that the one 'vexes the world' while the other 'pours balm upon it'. If we accept this view there would be no justification for describing Rabindranath Tagore as a philosopher. But the functions listed do not exhaust scope of philosophy. But in the wider sense of the term, philosophy includes nobility of conduct, richness of imagination, and depth of insight no less than clarity of thought. By this criterion, there should be no hesitation in describing Rabindranath Tagore as one of the important philosophers of the modern age. Philosophy to him, is the art of seeing, it is darshana. He is thus in tune with great thinkers who built up the philosophical tradition of India.[41] Tagore often refers to the two usual approaches i.e., intellectual approach and human approach full of feelings. Usually philosophers neglect one of them, particularly the latter one to sound highly impartial. In case of Tagore a conglomeration of both is seen visibly due to his humanistic convictions. He himself admits this when he declares, "I have great faith in humanity. Like the sun it can be clouded, but never extinguished...... We are waiting for the time when the spirit of age will be incarnated in a complete human truth and the meeting of men will be translated into the unity of man."[42] In all his passion for the human feelings and the omnipotence of Nature, he stresses the affinity between man and nature. Despite this Tagore does not rate lowly the advancement of spirit over Nature. He agrees that both are closely related but cannot be considered as equals. In 'Sadhana', Tagore says: "The revealment of the infinite is to be seen most fully not in the starry heavens but in the soul of man."[43] Tagore has ascribed the highest status to human-self because according to him the Almighty reveals Himself in a special manner. That is why he opposes the idea of a dichotomy accepted by many, between the Real and the Unreal. For the majority of the philosophers they should be ever recognized as opposites only. Tagore insists that everything has the germ of Reality. The way objects differ from each other signifies differences in their composition. Therefore, according to Tagore nothing is totally devoid of Reality or everything is real to some extent. He expresses this in Gitanjali.

"The song that was never completed,the butt that wited before blooming, the river that lost its track in the desert and failed to reach the ocean, I know, I know even these have not been altogether futile."[44] This is known as the doctrine of degrees which forces us to accept the reality of the lower. This is not to be thought as an attempt to bridge a gap that lies between the lower and higher forms of Reality.

It may be asserted that Rabindranath Tagore, an exponent of the Vedanta system, always stood for the synthetic idealism. This kind of idealism does not overlook the temporal and the finite. At the same time it projects its concentration mainly on the eternal spirit. This is where the realm of mysticism appears quite cognitive which otherwise always got enshrouded in a world other than the one we live in. Such a type of mysticism is referred as practical mysticism which is reflective in our behaviour. What is found as new in the theory is that it expects everybody to live and act in a temporal world but at the same time all efforts are directed to consecrate our actions. This in the opinion of Tagore is true humanistic idealism and a dedication to God. He conveys his feelings which are perfectly enveloped in spiritualism but bear a bedrock support from the humanistic level. This line of thinking has made Tagore to withstand the usual difficulties one finds in fixing up a stage for humanism. Majority religious philosophers have thoroughly magnified the spiritualistic demands that failed to treat humanistic level of comprehension with any regard. Tagore brings out this note in Gitanjali —

> " Oh grant me my prayer that I may never lose the bliss
> of the touch of the one in the play of the many."[45]

It is safe to clarify that unlike the usual concepts of Reality and God, wherein both are viewed as independent entities, Tagore's philosophy does not allow any such distinction. However, in metaphysics such a distinction is found necessary though Tagore disallows it completely. In his poems he may feel that such a differentiation is brought about automatically but his poems cannot be philosophically analysed. With his ardent support for the Sankara's Absolute he believes everything as a manifestation of the Absolute only. On this basis it may be concluded that Tagore allows his philosophy to get superimposed over the theistic beliefs. The only difficulty that lies with Tagore's philosophy is that while it maintains a theistic position, many a time it does try to expose the weakness or limitations of Abstract Monism and in general the Vedantic ideas. He has been, therefore, criticised for allowing the influence of Christianity. B.K. Lal stoutly refutes these charges.

"... Such accusations are not well-founded. Tagore can never even imagine that he is in any way contradicting Vedanta on the other hand, he is firmly of the opinion that the theistic emphasis is not so much on account of the influence of Christianity as on account of the other influences. The influence of Christianity might have been there, but it is almost insignificant in comparison to the tremendous influence which philosophers like Ramanuja and saints like Dadu and Kabir had on his theistic convictions."[46]

Tagore's explanation for the set of beliefs is very easy to understand and also convincing. His belief in a personal God has been founded on a perfect logic. It seems he has also considered the psychological aspect before arriving at this doctrine. Man, by nature, cannot generate interest unless he has an access to the object or atleast to its shades. This means that the report between what has been aimed and the subject aspiring for it is compulsory. Therefore, man can develop interest in only approachable objects. If God or Brahman are described in an abstract way or imagined as Nirguna Brahman (without attribute) then it is highly improbable for man to uphold the relationship. In his own words, "Just as the physiology of our beloved is not our beloved, so this impersonal law is not our God."[47] Hence Tagore's idealism has a premise in which both man and God live together. It is necessary to humanise even the Absolute otherwise everything will sound as only a loud claim. The species that built the relationship between man and God can only be through love. It is only the intense love which can fructify the relationship. Our God, has to be God and Man at the same time and, "If this faith be blamed for being anthropomorphic, then man is to be blamed for being man."[48] Even after speaking of the mutual relationship, the personal God, Tagore warily avoids the possibility of the finite merging into the infinite. Attribution of a personality does not limit God. Once anything is assigned the Divine status, Tagore thinks that it is free from the shortcomings observed in the human personality. Human personality has its own limitations due to wants desires, and defects. But the Divine personality is an 'infinite' personality which cannot be appraised on the usual meter of finitude. Therefore, Tagore does not appreciate designating the Infinite with certain qualities. This shows that Tagore is conscious of the fact that only at an illumined state man can have an actual inter-communion. In the course of enthusiasm which searched for an easily adoptable personality of God, Tagore stressed that the Infinite personality has to remain unaffected by the finiteness of the finite personalities. This is what prompts him to think. "There is a point where in the mystery of existence contradictions meet, where movement is not all stillness, where the idea and the form, the within and without, are united where infinite becomes finite without loosing its infinity."[49]

Such a feeling is an outcome of a superlogical personality because it may not fit into the normal formalities of logic.

Existence of God

After describing the Infinite personality as something absolutely exclusive Tagore feels that the usual proofs like Ontological, Teleological, Causal, Pragmatic, Empirical, Moral, Error, Deism, Pantheism, Panentheism and Theism need not be again referred to. This is because he does not want to create God out of logical conclusions, intellectual acrobatics, or conventional arguments. Tagore says that since God is a pre-requisite of existence, it is unwise to search for proofs or furnish some evidence. In spite of this Tagore knows that rational proofs and logical demonstrations do carry their own importance. Therefore, he also offers proofs for the existence of God. Some of them keep some resemblance with the traditional ones but the one based on the principle of joy has no parallel. One such argument supported by Tagore is the Teleological argument. To many of us it seems that every object in nature has some definite and well-defined purpose. This generally leads us to believe that there is God who has planned all the objects. Carefully many of the naturally occuring phenomena certainly lead us to believe in the existence of God who is making the universe run in order. Tagore, being a poet-philosopher examines everything through a twin angle. For him Nature and its beauty are of utmost importance. Similarly the harmony residing in the various Nature phenomena also attracts him. He has a firm belief in a power that governs these orderly phenomena. In the king of the Dark chamber, he expresses, this feeling —

"Look at the nice order and regularity prevailing all over the place-how do you explain it without a king."[50] Also in Creative Unity he points out : "We feel that this world is a creation, that in its centre there is a living idea, which reveals itself in an external symphony played on innumerable instruments, all keeping perfect tunes."[51] Therefore, Tagore trusts in the presence of a controller without whom it is not possible to have continuity in the harmony of the Nature-symphony. It would be the essential postulate for a doctrine which contemplates the existence of God. For Tagore, this could be the only reason as to why despite so many diversities we experience unity. However, what has been usually inferred by most of us does not tally with Tagore's claims. At this juncture Tagore explains the insufficiency of the point of views commonly held in picturising the world. The distorted picture of the world full of chaos and disorder, is not acceptable to Tagore. Like Spinoza, he thinks that truth does not lie in ordinary consciousness. Our gathering of knowledge has most of its part based on the empirical methods. Therefore, with limited capacity and insight what has been discerned could be at its best called as empirical knowledge. This would certainly throw light on a few aspects which might pose as complete in structure. The apparent gain in knowledge is nothing more than partial data. As Tagore imagines the spirit has thoroughly pervaded the world it would be a mistake to declare the world as full of disharmony or what has been sanctioned to us as just an entropean world. S. Radhakrishnan writes: "The whole universe is penetrated and vitalised by the living spirit and so responds to the call of spirit. Not a fragment of it which is not deeply interesting and divine, if we approach it in the right way. Anything can be made the channel of approach to God, an entrance to immortality. "All paths lead to thee', Nothing in the visible world is too low for the use of spirit. The dull dense world has openings throughout to the white radiance - God the great giver can open the whole universe to our grace in the narrow space of a single lane - Infinite is the mansion, my Lord. It is never too late to become a recruit to God's army."[52] Therefore, Tagore states that truth always lies in the consciousness of the whole but not in the consciousness of fragments. It means that it is the viewpoint that decides the existence of harmony of disharmony. A viewpoint which can look beyond the customary picture of the world can only provide a total picture of the world. It is in this regard that Tagore gives the example of the musicians who can produce melody through the strings of the instrument but for others who are devoid of that genius it is merely a set of wires being assembled. Therefore, to perceive the unity in diversity, a broad outlook is necessary.

Tagore does not stop with these proofs. Had it been so, he could have been considered as the true follower of one of the popular schools. The novelty lies in his suggestion which expects everyone to derive joy out of all creations. Tagore stresses this need because for him nothing could be erected without joy. Therefore, the fact of joy is inherent in every aspect of creation. Every individual within him has the capacity to feel this joy. Now, since the creation can exhibit joy, the creator must be himself a living principle of joy. This joy again should not be equated with pleasure because the principle of joy expects every person to derive joy from every creation but not to draw pleasure to satisfy self for baser means. It is for the sake of this point that Tagore clarifies certain terms which many a time go without any demarcation. Just as joy is different from pleasure, emotion and passion are also holding different meanings in Tagore's writings. Emotion has human nature and understanding while passion might be subjected to animal instinct. Pure joy appears to Tagore as having no other explanation except the fact that it is Divine.[53] He relies on the publicised experiences of the great saints and their style of living. No logic is applicable to analyse their lives. In 'Lover's gift and crossing' Tagore explains this fact.

"Dadu, Ravidas, Kabir and Nanak... had glimpses of the world unity... they babble like babes of the joy of their vision of Him, of the ecstasy into which His music has thrown them."[54]

Tagore does not totally rely on this kind of empirical argument which tries to prove existence of God on the basis of the experiences of the religious people. As per their character and integrity, their words have to be trusted. In addition to this Tagore presupposes God as an object or source of love, hope and aspiration. Every urge of ours in its genuine form needs firstly explanation and then satisfaction. This is possible only when our urges take shelter under the supreme. Thus the longing for the supreme, though unknown, has some meaning. It cannot be ruled out as something psychological. The very longing suggests the presence of the supreme behind these phenomena. Tagore, therefore, feels that it is quite necessary to hunt out the proofs of the existence of God. God has to be realised in any of the possible aspects depending upon our capacity. It is useless to waste time over the search for the logically satisfying evidences. In conclusion it may be said that Tagore's God, whom he calls Jivandevata, is a great lover, fountain of joy and supreme in every aspect. The wonderful part of his philosophy is that it also considers man and love external like God. Therefore, the pangs of separation are not only experienced by man alone but also by God, who has to quench the thirst for the company of the finites. This can be seen in his poem:

> "Thus it is that the Joy in me is so full. Thus it is that thou hast come down to me. O thou Lord of all heavens, where would be thy love if I were not? Thous hast taken me as thy partner of all this wealth. In my heart is the endless play of thy delight. In my life thy will is ever taking shape. And for this, thou who are the king of kings has decked thyself in beauty to captivate my heart. And for this thy love loses itself in the love of thy lower, and there art thou seen in the perfect union of two."[55]

The Problem of Evil

Although most of the philosophies that emerged from the theistic presumptions had the major aim of proving the existence of God, yet they could not afford to overlook the problem of evil. The usual proofs for the existence of God also included the qualities or characteristics of the supreme. The descriptions brought up the personality of God with total perfection and, therefore, it was neither possible nor desirable to attach limitations in any of the powers of the Almighty. Despite this the problem of evil even today continues with the same potency that it has carried formerly. It looks as if evil is equally eternal. Therefore, one of the most challenging tasks for the philosophers is to adjust this world morally. The common man's enquiry, 'If God is all good, why is there evil and suffering?' is not without qualifications Tagore prefers to tackle this age-old problem in his own way.

Tagore prefers to admit the existence of evil without calling it 'an illusion'. He even goes to the extent of accepting the factual existence of it in the finite world. However, what obsesses him is whether evil can be sanctioned eternity. Being a poet philosopher, he is more keen on proving the positive aspects of the supreme, like love, compassion, and joy. What irks him is that evil is also granted permanency in this finite world and is thus related to the incapacity of the supreme, who is certainly all powerful. He writes : "Pain which is the feeling of finiteness, is not a fixture in our life. It is not an end in itself as Joy is. To meet with it is to know what it has no part in the permanence of creation."[56] Again he says, "Evil cannot altogether arrest the course of life on the high way and rob it of its possessions. For the evil has to pass on, it has to grow into good; it cannot stand and give battle to All."[57] Therefore, what Tagore wants is that evil may be recognized but it should not be valued as something permanent. This is what the scheme of Reality demands. Tagore thinks that the creation has to be moulded properly so that it can transcend from the finiteness to the infiniteness. This creation is conditioned in such a way that while it takes up the journey from the finite world to the infinite, it has to learn to shed the evil and merge into the eternal joy. Whatever amount of pain that is carried by us shows our true wealth as imperfect Beings. The finite must realize own soulhood and this is why it has to tread through pain and suffering. Thus when it is said that the path is hard it means with every stride there is evil ready to attack. This is what is the precondition of the journey. Tagore in fact, whole heartedly accepts pain as a necessary corrective factor. Without it according to him it is impossible to dispel darkness, ignorance and mortality.

In 'Lover's Gift and Crossing', he writes:

> "Thou hast done well, my lover, thou has done well to send me thy fire of pain. For my incense never yields its perfume till it burns, and my lamp is blind till it is lighted.
>
> When my mind is numb, its torpor must be striken by thy love's lighting; And the very darkness that blots my world burns like a torch when set afire by thy thunder."[58]

Then comes the question as to how to combat with this evil? Having admitted its presence and capacity to weaken human will, yet Tagore believes in facing it with an intention of eradicating it. He suggests: "Come what may, have a strong mooring in your own self. Evils and pains will come and shake the foundation of life but never, never lose confidence."[59] What Tagore wants to suggest is that evil is a fact of the finite existence, and yet, existence itself is not an evil. Even then evil can pose the problem if it is granted permanency or final aspect of existence. Tagore asserts that the general way of looking at the evil is totally wrong. Since we infer evil as an isolated entity and forget the other aspects while doing so, it is automatically magnified. This is what is the fault with human judgement. At the most evil as an imperfection should be considered as a phase in which denial of the reality pervades. However, Tagore thinks that this route of imperfections and evils, is merely a platform leading to good or perfection. That is why Tagore prays:

> "Where the mind is without fear and head is held high; where knowledge is free; where the world has not broken up into fragments by narrow domestic walls;
>
> Where words come out from the depth of truth; Where tireless striving stretches its arms toward perfection; where the clear stream of reason has not lost its way into the dreary desert sand of dead habit; Where the mind is led forward by thee into ever widening thought and action; Into that heaven of freedom, my Father, let my country awake."[60]

This shows that Tagore is optimistic about the future. He wants an ardent trust in the powers of the supreme. He hates the negative aspects of life being usually given a status. He expects the very scheme or project of Reality to allow include these negations of life and therefore, referring to pessimism, suffering and death, he says: "Pessimism is a form of mental dispomania. It disdains healthy nourishment, indulges in the strong drink of denunciation and creates an artificial dejection which thirsts for a stronger draught."[61] Tagore is the first Indian thinker (according to Heiler) to whom the mystery of suffering in all its greatness has been revealed. Nothing is so contrary to Indian thought as the faith that suffering can be a revelation of God. To the Indian mind suffering is nothing more than the working out of the law of Karma, over which law, even the Gods have no control. Suffering is not the unavoidable consequence of human deeds as the law of Karma asserts but a means to divine grace a painful means through which God draws man to himself. The burden of pain is a gift of God. Since suffering comes from the hands of a loving God, it is for the good men a source of imperishable joy. Death is neither painful nor terrible. Its sting has been drawn and it is gate into eternal life. Death is nothing but a change in the arms of God. Death is God's messenger and therefore, the friend of man."[62]

Basic Features of Tagore's Philosophy

It may be concluded that firstly Tagore adopts a synoptic approach according to which philosophy is as much a matter of experience as of idealism. He has been successful in naturally retaining throughout his works an aesthetic approach to the philosophical questions. A philosopher who has the knack of inquiry through the metaphysics culminating from the poetic imagination, can certainly deal with the problems through the gateway of art. Tagore has combined religion, philosophy and art to synthesize his philosophy to suit the modern mind. Secondly, he often deals with philosophical issues in their inter-relatedness. That is why he does not eliminate living realities, even though they appear to be harsh realities. Thirdly, he emphasises in the reconciliation of the elements of value which might be appearing extremely divergent in their stand points. V.S. Narvane, describes it as "... Whether he is speaking of metaphysical theories or of religious traditions, of ethical doctrines or of social attitudes, he focusses attention on the common meeting ground rather than the barrier which divides representatives of different persuasions. A poetic expression of this attitude is seen in the following lines:

> "Feeling seeks to embody itself in form And
> Form is for ever abandoning itself to feelings.
>
> The Infinite longs for the finite's close com-
> radeship while the finite desires to lose itself
> in the Infinite.
>
> In creation and dissolution, through some mys-
> terious contrivance
>
> There is an eternal coming and going between
> the outer and the inner.
>
> Bondage is in search of its own freedom
> And freedom begs for a dwelling - place within
> bondage."[63]

Yet another aspect introduced or rather supported by Tagore is the 'Middle Path' theory in his philosophy. In fact, the concept cannot be treated as something new but the way Tagore has persented it, is slightly different. For the critics the very idea that underlines the Middle path philosophy is quite confusing.

They even term it as a sign of intellectual confusion. This kind of philosophy was encouraged by the Buddha, but the Madhyam Marga as it was enunciated in sermons does not expect the evading attitude towards the extremities and seek stability somewhere in the middle. Critics feel that this could be a sort of retreat or escape. On the other hand it is very positive and that is why tries to select the best of the extremities. In doing so, this theory certainly deletes the unsatisfactory parts in each camp. When Tagore tries to build the personality with the anticipation of a descend of Divinity he has to recommend the 'Middle Path' theory. Therefore, he interprets the infinite in terms of finite experience but does not gloss over the distinction between the Infinite and the Finite. This shows that although Tagore declares that he relies on scriptures, he seems to view the infinite through his sense organs and through the finite only. "This arbitrary fixation of locus to judge the external world and internal personality has led him to accept a bi-polar infinite and a bi-polar finite, and the everlasting world of creation as a joint effort. Being immersed in the central unity, the poet, or the artist creates. Even in the unitary act of creation Tagore is not prepared to ignore the dual nature of reality."[64]

However, Tagore does not clarify the mystery which causes difference in various degrees between the finites. It becomes necessary to sum up by saying that the poet philosopher had indicated in his poems and philosophy, the need for freedom and craze for Nature. As he seldom speaks of a poet's religion as something different from that of a philosopher's religion, he wants to point out everywhere God's creation as unique though the premises would change. It may be concluded that Tagore's philosophical sketches though remain expressive, mainly, in the poetic form yet do not depart from the Hindu tradition. The religious movements gave Tagore a new avenue to bring out the best of the existing tradition and coagulate the same with the intention of establishing a firm platform. This could further accommodate the metaphysical standpoint, which was missing in most of the social philosophies. This is the reason why Tagore does not weaken the Upanisadic connections. In the opinion of V.S. Narvane,

"The Hindu tradition influenced Rabindranath Tagore mainly through the Upanisads and through the medieval theistic religious movements. Some of his essays may be described as commentaries on themes derived from the Upanisads and many of his poems are based upon Upanisadic parables or dialogues. However, it should be remembered that he did not turn to them in order to find support for any pre-conceived metaphysical or ethical theory. The absolutistic interpretation of the Upanisads given by the advaita school did not appeal him. He felt closer to the theistic Upanisads given by the advaita school did not appeal him. He felt closer to the theistic Upanisads like Isa and Svetasvatara rather than to those like Katha, Chhandogya and Brihadaranyaka in which the identity of the Absolute with the self is the dominant idea. Rabindranath Tagore was one of the first to point out that Western scholars had given a distorted picture by emphasising the ideas of illusion, sorrow and ascetism in the Upanisads."[65]

Symbolic representation is an exclusive art of poets. Tagore, the poet-philosopher, utilizes this for explaining the ultimate stage in the process of life. For Tagore, harmony is the only aim and crux of life. He imagines in all his poems, life with harmony. Humanity in its perfect shape can boast of spirituality and this could be realized while living only. He does not believe in shifting the proper aims of humanity in a purely metaphysical world. That is why we often come across his intrinsic persuasion through his writings which propose exempts from Nature:

Tagore conveys his *philosophy of harmony* through his favourite symbol of the river. Eternally the same and eternally new, the river-seems to symbolise the co-existence of apparently opposite principles. Here are the concluding lines of the poem Prabahini, Vol. Purabi in which the personified river describes her own career.

A stream of darkness fills my heart
A stream of light my eyes
My dance belongs to the mortal earth
My songs to heaven rise

To my right is happiness
Pain to my left attends
In the tranquil sea of music
Melody's journey ends. "[66]

Tagore is one of the rare philosopher, who has dared to correct the acknowledged rational knowledge by intuition. This method is certainly unusual and not easily acceptable. However, philosophical judgements in view of Tagore do not seem to be really free from rational thinking and therefore, a reversible trend may be expected. This does not mean that he puts intuition well ahead of the rational knowledge.

"On the question of knowledge, Tagore emerges as a rationalist who is not afraid of enriching Reason by Intuition. In ethics he sees an elements of value in activistic humanism, but is also deeply aware of the dangers of 'work intoxication'. In religion, he accepts bhakti but is careful not to identify himself with the cult of ecstasy."[67]

SWAMI VIVEKANANDA (1862-1902)

In order to understand the philosophy of Vivekananda, it is necessary to refer to Sri Ramkrishna Paramhansa who infused a philosophical discipline in his mind. As a saint of Dakshinesvar, Ramkrishna occupies a decisive position in the formation of Indian thought. Coming from a well-to-do family, Vivekananda did not have his early life eventful. He was a keen student of Indian scriptures as well as Western thought. It appears that his early mental outlook owed much to rationalistic, sceptic and agnostic thinking. It was only in 1881 when he met his master-Guru-his entire mental disposition experienced a dramatic change. Nevertheless, he did not easily submit to the mystical teachings of Ramkrishna. Vivekananda, who was destined to be the true apostle of his master steadily discovered the genuine spiritual order in his master. Ramkrishna taught him the truth of Advaita which was reinterpreted to suit the modern world. In fact like Socrates, Ramkrishna was a person who without any innovations, without founding a cult or even contributing anything strikingly original to the sum of human knowledge acted as an inspirer of much that was of enduring value. [68]

It was Vivekananda's inquisitiveness that drew the required knowledge from Ramkrishna and in turn encouraged him to reinterpret the essence of Advaita. What Ramkrishna taught him was not something new but that of Adi Sankara's teachings. This is because Ramkrishna had a firm faith in Advaita, which he termed as the real culmination of all spiritual disciplines towards which all religious strivings are directed. This is the reason as to why we find that Vivekananda's writings are pregnant with the most essential features of the ideologies of the 19th and early 20th centuries. The writings are searchlight for further development. At an early age Vivekananda studied John Stuart Mill, Descartes, Spinoza, Hume, Kant, Fichte, Hegel, Schopenhauer, Comte and Darwin. He closely observed the developments of social affairs in Europe. Owing to these influences and his personal tragic experiences he could grasp the different and practical meanings of life. His experience led him to re-estimate some of the values which he held in high esteem. As such, he discovered the living truths in a simple way. He was very much disturbed by the fact that in real life, the weak, the poor, and the abandoned never had any place. That is why he raised voice against the Indian bourgeois ideology prevalent at that time and expressed his concern for the mass.

Vivekananda's Basic Philosophical Status

There is no denying the fact that Vivekananda was inspired by his desire to re-orient the Vedanta philosophy. Therefore, he attempted to delve into the material that helped flourish the philosophical heritage of India. His major works, i.e., Vedanta philosophy. The Vedanta in all its phases, the Vedanta philosophy and Christianity, Hints on practical spirituality, and Karma Yoga contain a perfect critique of the erstwhile Vedantic interpretations of basic philosophical problems and inquiry. The concept of Vedanta philosophy appealed him so much that he considered it as a reservoir of all the orthodox and unorthodox philosophical trends in India. He asserted that Vedanta and Hinduism should be considered as synonymous. In this connection, he observes : "Thus the Vedanta, whether we know it or not, has penetrated all the sects in India, and what we call Hinduism....has been throughout interpreted by the influence of the Vedanta. Whether we are conscious of it or not, we think the Vedanta, we live in the Vedanta, we breathe the Vedanta, and we die in the Vedanta and every Hindu does that ..." [69] Thus, it is obvious that Vivekananda entirely relied upon Vedanta or Upanisads in order to interprete the philosophical traditions and to point out their relation to the modern period. Nevertheless, it would be wrong to say that his work is confined to the ideas of Vedanta since he also referred to his early ideas gathered from the Western philosophical writings. He always tried to prune the ancient philosophical reserves to build up a new stable model. He was disturbed by the old way of presentation and as such he attempted to obtain a single current which eventually became a new basic of Vedanta. He wrote : "This is my attempt, my mission in life to show that the Vedantic schools are not contradictory, that they all necessitate each other, all fulfil each other, and one, as it were, is the stepping stone to the other."[70] Therefore, at the outset Vivekananda classified the contemporary Vedantist trends into two groups, viz., the dualist and the non-dualist. The former adhered to the philosophy of Ramanuja while the latter was represented by Sankara. It must be borne in mind that these two schools had totally opposite views with regard to the existence of the world. Vivekananda pointed out that the meanings of dualism and non-dualism expressed by Vedanta were quite different from those understood by the European Schools at that time. The very concept of dualism according to Vivekananda should include recognition of the two worlds, the phenomenal and the world-where Brahman is the wholesole. The usual clash between matter and spirit is taken up by the western scholars as a clue to understand the existence of duality in the universe. Vivekananda is the first philosopher who points out that the division between matter and spirit leads to a defective theory as both of them dwell together. He insisted that they should not be treated under different headings since both of them form the important party of the phenomenal world. However, they may be viewed as different phases of the same entity. Hence, matter remains in a crude form while spirit assumes a fine form. It is on this principle that Vivekananda tries to ignore the age-old strife between the philosophers of materialism and idealism. In fact this idea without any pretence of scientific analysis of the phenomenal world shows concurrence. The scientific analysis shows that matter and energy go hand in hand, while Vivekananda's interpretation carries matter and spirit together. He observes : "One party says, thought is caused by matter, and the other says, matter is caused by thought. Both statements are wrong; matter and thought are co-existent. There is a third something (Brahman-Atman), of which both matter are products. "[71] Therefore, Vivekananda does not uphold a division within the nature. When we presume certain aspects as external or internal it does not mean that they have different source. The external aspects are easily exhibited and therefore, they may fall into the line of activism while the internal aspects affixed to the root and therefore have little scope to propagate the force within them. According to Vivekananda it is wrong to say that matter and spirit or matter and mind are independent or objects having contrary tendencies. He cites the examples of our day-to-day life and attempts to substantiate his argument that matter and mind are just forces which spring from the same source. Moreover, both have the same root. He says : "The very fact that the external force can somehow evoke the external force shows that somewhere they join each other-they must be continuous and therefore, basically the same force.... Since the same force appears in one form as matter and in another form as mind, there is no reason to think matter and mind are different. Mind is changed into matter, matter is changed into mind."[72] Having pointed out that everything is an outcome of the same reality, Vivekananda also introduces the principle of interconvertibility in nature as the scientists have done. Thus, the whole universe comprises of so many types of of matter and which form is regarded of utmost importance is immaterial. To substantiate this point it can be said that nature is homogeneous in character. What has been discerned by intellect as fragments is due to differentiation, which is only in manifestation. The Vedantists use the Sanskrit word Prakriti to denote nature which literally means differentiation. Finally mind and matter experience the interconvertibility because of the process of vibration.

It is important to note that though Vivekananda makes clarification of various points and cites number of examples, still his philosophy has not been given due weightage in materialism or idealism. Vivekananda seems to have focussed his attention on these two schools. Therefore, very often he expresses the view that the existing struggle between materialism and idealism is a result of deep misunderstanding. He also hints that this conflict should be attributed to the faulty reasoning. Thus, Vivekananda's enthusiasm to rise above materialism and idealism has led him to adopt a totally different line of philosophy which could be designated as a third line in the sphere of philosophy. The critics describe Vivekananda's view as erroneous since they have failed to properly realise the subsistence of his philosophy. The dualists usually attempt to eliminate the fundamental question of philosophy, and thereby try to rise above the clash between materialism and idealism. Probably Vivekananda's voracious reading of the Eastern and Western philosophies and his efforts to keep himself in tune with the scientific developments led him to adopt this view. Thus, it appeared to him that a third line in philosophy is quite possible in future.

Looking at his efforts, one gathers the impression that Vivekananda was simultaneously drawn to spiritualism and the rigorous activistic principle. He had therefore, no other alternative than to synthesize the essence of the theories of the opposing schools, and overlook the minor points of difference. We are familiar with the Vedantic outlook, which considers this world as Maya or illusory and unreal. Therefore, Vedantists discard any theory related to the 'reality' of the world. Vivekananda on the other hand came out openly and forcefully to lift this world to a 'reality'. This was for the first time when someone really attempted to re-establish an accommodative doctrine. He writes , 'All religions teach that this world is nothing. Beyond this world is something which is very real. Here comes the difficulty......to believe that mind is all, that thought is all, is only a higher materialism." [73] In fact, it is objective idealism which leads him to reconsider both materialism and idealism. He does not agree with the view that the Reality is something which is beyond the purview of this world. He holds that since everything has been the result of the Brahman, it is illogical to argue that we live in a world which is full of illusions. He also condemns the bias view of both materialism and idealism and pleads for a strong ground to his objective idealism, which is regarded as his basic philosophy.

World and its Creations

Vivekananda's philosophic endeavours aimed at the re-arrangement of the Advaita Vedanta in an intelligible and scientific manner. Perhaps, this might have been the need of the hour at that time which led him to rehearse his master's teachings. His philosophical writings indicate the level of his multisided perfection. They go far beyond the confines of religion and philosophy. Vivekananda starts with the fundamental and significant questions about the world. The questions that have really puzzled most of the philosophers are regarding the nature, origin and creation of the world. In fact, there are various theories which attempt to explain these phenomena. It seems that Vivekananda's ideas run parallel to that of Sankara's presumptions.

Brahman is considered to be the absolute, stable and eternal. As far as his characteristics are concerned, Brahman remains Nirguna-without qualities. Brahman occupies the universe and is amorphous in nature. As such he is regarded infinite. However, Brahman should be attested by the nature as being the only cause of this universe. The Vedantists argue that the gap between the Brahman and the Universe is purely metaphysical. Brahman is also imagined to be devoid of qualities and is also defined relatively in the phenomenal world. It is transient, finite, dynamic and possessing form. Therefore, what has been described as Saguna with attributes is also considered as reality. Nevertheless, it is difficult to fill the metaphysical gap between the Brahman and the Universe. As a matter of fact, Sankara's philosophy does not admit any creation though it does not disown the empirical point of view to study the process of creation. This view appears to be valid only from a non-transcendental angle. In fact, Vivekananda attempted to maintain a balance between these two views. Having recognised the world as reality he resorted to the basics of the Vedanta system-the monistic position, and explained the impasse by saying that the former is an aspect of the latter. This does not imply that Vivekananda somehow wants to perpetuate both the views. On the other hand he insists on the state of realisation where the usual distinction between the creator and the created world does not exist. However, like a dualist he also points out the necessity of acknowledging the existent world as real only. Therefore, the creation as suggested by him appears to be a reflection of the genius of the creator-the infinite-which is cognized by us as the world-the finite. Thus even the Infinite needs the finite medium to express itself. Despite this, it is usually thought that the Infinite itself assumes either the form of finite or becomes finite. If this change is accepted, then the very philosophy of Sankara or even that of Vivekananda may sound hypothetical. Vivekananda was foresighted enough to anticipate these differences and hence he explains them with an illustration. He writes: "Here is the Absolute (a), and this is the universe (b). The Absolute has become the universe. By this is not only meant the material world but the mental world, the spiritual world-heavens and earths, and in fact, everything that exists. Mind is the name of a change and body the name of another, and so on, and all these changes compose our universe. The Absolute (a) has become the universe (b) by passing through time, space and causation (c)."[74]

The *diagram* shows that the Absolute and the universe are separated by certain parameters and they are independent. However, the Absolute cannot descend to the level of the Universe without passing through time, space and causation. The absolute does not possess any of these forms. In this regard, Space indicates position, Time generates thought and Causation introduces duality i.e., the presence of two entities. Since Absolute is considered extremely stable it cannot be subjected to change and due to its perfect nature it has to be even without a position. Thus, it is obvious that the Absolute is imagined to be

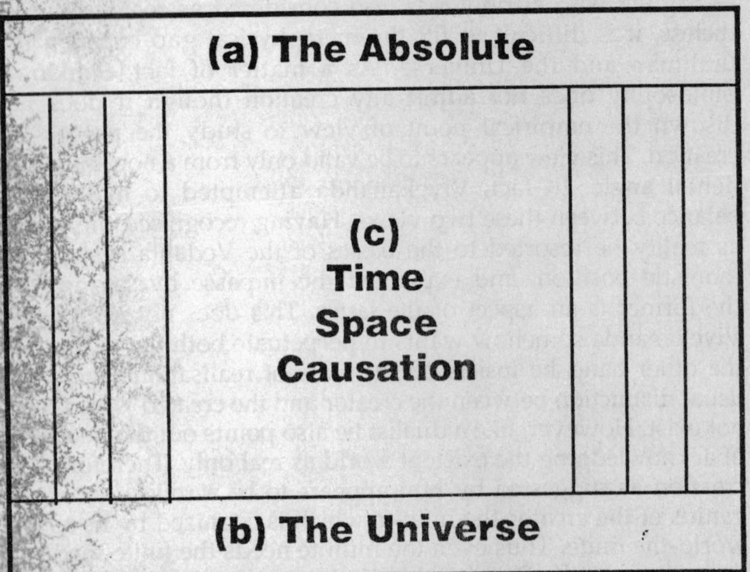

free from the usual modes of description. It can be said that unless the process of creation commences it is impossible for the time, space and causation to operate. Therefore, one must bear in mind all these in order to study the process. Nevertheless the questions which arise are like where from these three emerge? What causes their emergence? Are they the independent entities? Vivekananda appears to have predicted these difficulties as he pleads only for the Absolute and the Universe. In case of the entities, he prefers to call them as mere forms rather than the metaphysical realities. This indicates that they do not have independent existence. Time is entirely dependent on our mind. The very idea of time as recognized by our mind implies periods or span of a certain duration. If the time is not recognised as independendent the space also loses its ground. The dimensions of space also have to be recognised by our vision. Similarly, whenever we recognize something as effect, it must have a cause and vice-versa. In fact, it is the mind which has to identify them. Therefore, they cannot be held as metaphysical realities. Vivekananda holds that these values should not be explained in the abstract manner as they cannot be accepted in the abstract form. They do need a concrete form, which demands dependency. These forms are of great importance because if God desires any creation, they are necessary and only through them one can get the results. That is why Vivekananda gives them an unusual status. That is why Vivekananda gives them an unusual status. Although, they are not realities in the metaphysical sense, yet, they cannot be treated as unreal or false. Vivekananda illustrates this with the help of the analogy of ocean and waves. He says: "The Waves are the same as the Ocean and yet they are different. But when the waves subside, the forms vanish, this does not mean that forms of the waves are illusory. So long as the waves exist, the forms are there, and one is bound to see the forms. This analogy explains the ground on which Vivekananda asserts the reality of the world. World with its forms of space, time and causation is not a delusion. In materialism these forms may vanish as do the forms of the waves when the waves subside, but so long as the world is there, these forms are there and one is bound to 'see them".[75] Thus, it is obvious that Vivekananda lays stress on the reality of the world and its constituents. Having slightly deviated from Sankara's philosophy, he explains in detail the duality. Sankara having mentioned monistic view throughout his philosophy overcomes the difficulty by calling the world as nothing but Jagat Mithya. Strongly enough, Vivekananda who disagrees with the Vedanta concept, maintains that Vedanta interpretations lack the proper explanation and nothing else. Unlike the other philosophers who plead for the correction of the source philosophy, Vivekananda upholds Sankara's philosophy with a view to reinterpret it and to overcome the shortcomings. He points out that creation and evolution are intimately connected and as such there is continuous process of creation. The Universe has to be considered as a real manifestation or what is usually termed as a perfectual creation. The three forms are always necessary for the manifestation.

Vivekananda and Schopenhauer

The life span of Arthur Heinrich Schopenhauer (1788-1860) witnessed a period of unusual philosophical activity in Germany. This was because scholars of international repute like - Kant, Fichte, Hegel, Schelling, Feurbach and Marx profusely wrote during this period. Schopenhauer's ideas centre round the views expressed by Kant and Hegel. He wrote his doctoral dissertation on Kant's theory of knowledge which served a blow to Hegel's optimistic view of the world history. He indicates his deep animosity towards Hegel and reverence for Kant's 'Critique of Pure Reason' in "The world as Will and Idea". He points out that the metaphysical system to be presented needs rather a balanced structure of thought and it is not proper to lable it with some common system of nomenclature. In order to develop its view, every system has to traverse against the existing intellectual organisation of the world. Schopenhauer's philosophy is not an exception to this. Schopenhauer's philosophy at present is regarded as a subdued and highly pessimistic kind of philosophy which draws out the living force of activity from life, purveying negation to even illogical heights and speculating the dominance of gloom forever. Schopenhauer, no doubt, shepherd a thought which is usually tainted as full of negative attributes, yet saw a release out of it. He does not just point out the world which lacks spirit but shows what causes such a world. At the initial stage of his philosophy he attempts to indicate the true structure of the world in which there is more pain than pleasure and more evil than good. While ensuring the causes for the disorder in the self and outside, he says that it is illogical to consider the world as 'good'. He is inclined towards the Upanisadic and Buddhistic philosophical writings to obtain some salvation. Thus, the eastern point of view may not present a pure theory in the sense, evolving out of Upanisads but it certainly gives a new expression leading to the same goal. Nietsche, the intellectual apostle and the pupil of Schopenhauer remarks about his master:

> "What he taught is put aside;
> What he lived, that will abide -
> Behold a man:
> Subject he was to none".[76]

Schopenhauer's philosophy for a brief survey may be divided into two parts i.e., The World as Idea and The World as Will. In the World as Idea Schopenhauer shows that the form of all human knowledge of the world is based upon the subject - object theory. There is no possibility to know this world or any other world except by being present to it as subjects. Therefore, it is amiss to think of subject without object and similarly object does not gather any meaning without being linked to the subject. Schopenhauer claims that the general structure of the objects of human experience are due to a principle within the knowledge of the subject itself. Thus according to Schopenhauer the principle of sufficient reason has three aspects. viz., space, time and causality. Space determines spatial dimensions, time promotes the temporal continuity of objects and causality binds space and time in a material activity. This proves that Schopenhauer does not take into consideration the concepts of the Absolute, the universe and the space while separating them. Unlike, Vivekananda, he does not represent his ideas in a schematic figure form. Schopenhauer described the world without relying upon the religious ideas. He allows everyone to grasp the world phenomenon as per his intellectual capacity since the principle of sufficient reason is anterior to the knowing activity of a subject. It is literally true for any man to say, "The World is my Idea". Hence the doctrine of world as idea does not constitute the whole of Schopenhauer's thesis of the world. He also wants to show the world as Will. However, to realise the world as idea he suggests the best image as only dream. When we dream, a world is produced within us. The notion accommodates space, time and material objects in our dream world. He observes: "The Vedas and Puranas have no better similie than a dream for the whole knowledge of the actual world, which they call the web of Maya, and they use none more frequently. Plato often says that men live only in a dream; the philosopher alone strives to awake himself."[77] Therefore, what has been said by Schopenhauer is keeping with the traditions but overtaking the canonical forms of truth.

Besides, while dealing with 'The World as Will' Schopenhauer critically examines the substance of the world. Usually, philosophers persistently attempt to find out the real substance of the world. They very often make claims on matter or subject only. In this regard Schopenhauer differs from them by introducing "Will". Vivekananda strongly criticises this view while pointing out that Schopenhauer has failed to understand the Vedanta philosophy on a decisive point.[78] But for Schopenhauer the core of reality cannot be matter because matter requires some form for its existence. Thus, matter has phases, conditions and qualities. He goes to the extent of saying that ultimately matter is the outcome of cause and effect. It is an ordered motion on a disciplined variety. Hence, it can be said that matter exists only by knowing a subject and it has no independent existence. The principle of sufficient reason exhibits the whole reality, while most of the philosophical theories presume that subject is the true kernel of all reality and it exists in itself. Schopenhauer denies this as he holds that this view would separate subject from object and make subject as the cause of all objects. To avoid the confusion arising due to the intellectualisation of various problems, he prefers 'Will' as the last resort.

While elaborating this, he says that man in all his walks of life experiences the force of Will and therefore, the whole existing reality is nothing but the objection of a single striving Will. The continuous and endless striving which seems to have manifested everywhere has no specific reason but itself. Will alone is the thing-in-itself. He points out that the core of reality is Will and therefore, the world is also Will. It is obvious that like early Greek philosophers, Schopenhauer also attempts to define the world with a single entity. As he connects every aspect of human life to 'Will' or the 'Willing process'. In this connection, Vivekananda does not agree with Schopenhauer and remarks that, Schopenhauer eliminates the very basic postulate of life the joy or the verve of life and reduces the whole life to a despondent picture. Schopenhauer insists, "All Willing arises from want, therefore, from deficiency, and therefore, from suffering. The satisfaction of a wish ends it; yet for one wish that is satisfied there remain at least ten which are denied. Further, the desire lasts long, the demands are infinite; the satisfaction is short and scantily measured out. But even the final satisfaction is itself only apparent; every satisfied wish at once makes room for a new one; both are illusions... No attained object of desire can give lasting satisfaction, but merely a fleeting gratification."[79] Probably Schopenhauer derives the essence of his philosophy from the Upanisads and then measures it with a pragmatic view. On account of this he might have been subjected to criticism despite the fact that he also sought the support of Buddhism.

While Vivekananda could not afford to appreciate such an attempt, mainly because of the then need of the hour in India.

In fact Schopenhauer's period was pregnant with German pessimism and Vivekananda's period was in a dire need of optimism. Therefore, both remain as the champions of the same cause, however, they strived to present it through different angles. Their source of inspiration was also the same. Nevertheless on the one hand, Schopenhauer's pessimistic approach is undermined as it leads to the negation in life and on the other hand, Vivekananda's unchecked optimism appears to be fading rapidly in the changing world. Thus, Vivekananda neither completely sticks to the traditional Vedanta nor thoroughly departs from it. He may be regarded as a neo-Vedantin who imports the knowledge of Vedanta and then subordinates it to the philosophical and moral obligations.

The Soul Theory

Vivekananda has concentrated in his philosophy on the nature, function and destiny of the soul. At the outset he prefers recommending some of the characteristics to the soul as innate. One such quality is freedom that speaks of the essence of the soul. It is,therefore, clear that soul as such cannot be bound by anything or is free from the bondage. While it is generally held that it has to express itself through bondage only. Vivekananda explains that the bondage as commonly understood is only apparent. However, Vivekananda's assumptions also are not without difficulties. Since antiquity it is presumed that soul is the suffering individual that does not possess sufficient capacity to perform all the desired actions. Owing to this Vivekananda has gone into detail to work out the destiny of the soul. In fact, just as the existence of God with the supposed attributes, at times causes doubts, similarly, the soul theory also has some lacunas. Vivekananda does not eliminate either but seeks to maintain a philosophical balance. He solves the problem by describing immortality as the basic quality of the soul. Nevertheless, he cautions that unless this is realised it is not possible to describe properly the capacities of the soul. Thus Vivekananda believes that the ultimate human destiny is this realisation. However, in this regard the very first difficulty faced by most of the persons is how to demonstrate the immortality of the soul? This is obvious because since the soul is free from bondage, it cannot fall in the premises where the scientific laws govern. Another difficulty is that if it cannot be proved to have the immortality by scientific means, it would fall into the unscientific notion. Therefore, the problem of immortality cannot be satisfactorily solved by rational analysis or justifications. Therefore, Vivekananda resorts to the Sankhya theory and then develops his point of view. Having reconsidered the earlier opinions, he says: "Out of all these various opinions rose Sankhya philosophy, where at once we find immense differences. The idea there is that man has first this gross body; behind the gross body is the fine body, which is the vehicle of the mind, as it were; and behind even that is the self, the perceiver, as the Sankhyas call it, of the mind; and this is omnipresent that is, your soul, my soul, everyone's soul is everywhere all the same time. If it is formless how can it be said to occupy space? Everything that occupies space has form. The formless can only be infinite."[80] In this connection, it is necessary to explain the meaning of the word 'Immortality', Vivekananda provides two literal meanings which cover the individual and the universal view. We know that immortality is connected to deathlessness. Another way of explaining it is that the state of death as usually understood, brings an end to the living being. The soul remains intact by this state or easily escapes it. Nonetheless, this explanation is regarded as negative though it is universally accepted. Vivekananda knew the areas where objections could be anticipated. The possibility lies where the concrete or positive form is granted with specifications. As ever he prefers to rely upon the Vedanta philosophy for clarifying such doubts, though the basic meaning is acceptable to him. Having considered the forthcoming issues and their consequences, he says: "That which does not die cannot live. For life and death are the obverse and reverse of the same coin. Life is another name for death, and death for life. One particular mode of manifestation is what we call life; another particular mode of manifestation of the same thing is what we call death. When the wave rises on the top of it is life; and when it falls into the hollow it is death. If anything is beyond death, we naturally see it must also be beyond life. I must remind you of the first conclusion that the soul of man is part of the cosmic energy that exists, which is God. We now find that it is beyond life and death... What is there, I ask to limit anything that is beyond law, beyond causation."[81] Therefore, Vivekananda wants to strengthen the doctrine of the soul with the help of his doctrines of ignorance and Karma. According to him the soul performs actions due to or in ignorance with the force of tendencies which become the efficient cause. Even then one cannot determine the ultimate nature of immortality so easily. The ultimate destiny could be known only when the birth-death cycle is finally smothered at some stage. This is keeping in with the wisdom of the ancient Indian philosophers who also held the similar view. Even if immortality is suggested to be the property of the soul, anybody would hardly agree that it is a goal to be achieved by persistent efforts. Vivekananda asserts that the soul is capable of achieving immortality because basically it is immortal. Although immortality is latent in it, however, the soul does not realise this due to ignorance. He remarks: "The whole of the manifestation of this one series, from the protoplasm upto the most perfect man, must be the very same thing as cosmic life. First it got involved and became finer, and out of that fine something; which was the cause, it has gone on evolving, manifesting itself, and becoming grosser... there is nothing new, there will be nothing new. The same series of manifestations are presenting themselves alternately like a wheel coming up and down."[82] By this Vivekananda wants to show that from the lowest protoplasm to the perfect living being, life is same. In addition, immortality is the consummation of the growth of man which implies that from the beginning to the end, it is the same basic being expressing itself.

The Path of Realisation and Karma Yoga

One of the apparent difficulties observed in the proposed theory of immortality of the soul, is that of knowing the path that can lead to immortality. Since man's intellect initially suspects and is more inclined to doubt any of the claims, it is customary to provide evidences to satisfy it. Therefore, it becomes essential to find out the way by which soul can realise immortality. Nothing fructifies without being subjected to a process. Every process in itself has multiple stages that looks highly compact, is Yoga. This word, in Indian philosophy, is normally associated with a dual meaning. The usual meaning is union, while the other one is discipline. Since yoga finds much of its scope viable in the field of spirituality, the latter meaning is considered as workable and the former as literal. Vivekananda incorporates both the meanings in his theory as he believes that unless this is done, the aspects of Yoga cannot be understood.

Thus, the path leading to the realization comprises of discipline and union. In fact, the term Yoga has variety of meanings. Vivekananda recommends a synthesis of all the meanings. As it is not possible for all those who seek the realisation to follow the same path, they choose according to their capacity, and the one suitable to their temperament. As such none, can be regarded as the supreme. Owing to this, we have Jnana Yoga, Karma Yoga, Raja Yoga and Bhakti Yoga which are the important limbs of Yoga. It is incorrect to say that they are incompatible with each other. Jnana Yoga is the Yoga of knowledge, Karma Yoga is the Yoga of action, Raja Yoga is the Yoga of psychology and Bhakti Yoga is the Yoga of devotion. They seek to achieve the same goal despite they follow the different approaches. Since human temperament, disposition and capacity vary, it is necessary to have various ways. A detail study of these paths shows that they complement each other and none of them has own exclusive characteristics.

From these types or rather positions, Vivekananda formulates the content and meaning of man's life, because basically man is nature's slave. But when he becomes free, nature becomes his slave. To avoid the possible quandary, Vivekananda writes: "The awakening of the soul to its bondage and its efforts to stand up and assert itself - this is called life."[83] Vivekananda is quite confident that ultimately he would succeed. He expressed that slavery would be eradicated and the hindrances in the path of salvation, Nirvana and freedom could be removed if the principles of any of the Yogas are adopted.

Karma Yoga

One of the vital concepts of Hinduism is that of liberation. Liberation as explained by most of the Indian philosophers somehow continues to remain as something like desire and aim of the soul.The soul on its own accord cannot easily or instantly free itself from the bondage. The screen of ignorance is quite intense and can be annuled with the assistance of knowledge only. The full mind implies a perfect one and its internal structure comprises of philosophy mysticism, emotion and work. These four elements should be in a perfect and balanced form. This could be successfully attained by Yoga. It is pointed out: "To the worker, it is union between himself and the whole of community; to the mystic, union between his lower self; to the lower, union between himself and the God of love; and to the philosopher, the unity of all existence."[84] One who strives and endures to achieve this ideal is called a Yogi. The four parts Karma, Bhakti, Raja and Jnana correspond to the worker, the devotee, the mystic and the philosopher respectively.

Vivekananda asserts that the four Yogas do not conflict with each other. In spite of this, he has often emphasised on Karma-Yoga, not just because it suits a vast majority but it was the demand of the hour. However, the clash between philosophy and science or idealism and materialism continues to remain in the same spirit. The Indian philosophy especially the ancient one has been subjected to criticism on the ground that it is pessimistic and highly fatalistic. Every follower of this philosophy aims at the spiritual gains and therefore, harbours only the idealistic values.Owing to this he is bound to give room for inaction, or escape from the duties. Although attempts have been made to indicate that escapism or inaction has no place in Indian philosophy, yet everyone will have to accept its pessimism regarding the problems of life and life after death. This is obvious from the fact that renunciation was never understood in the metaphysical sense and resigning from the duties was equated to the release of the soul from the bondage. The bondage was credited with the chief cause of suffering. The world was always imagined to be a club of negative qualities and the positive ones to be achieved in a world other than this. Therefore, it is wrong to blame westerners for their failure to grasp the real substance. On the other hand the interpretors should be blamed for relating idealism, to pessimism and pessimistic attitude to the living principles. Owing to this western writers while writing the books on the history of philosophy do not take the note of the Indian philosophy and even comment that it does not deserve any place. Hence Vivekananda had to rise to the occasion in order to provide the true knowledge and guidance. While giving little more importance to Karma Yoga, Vivekananda succeeded in pointing out that even before the beginning of the western philosophies, Indian philosophy paid attention to these problems and made suggestions in the light of metaphysics. Due to the neglect towards fame, the true wisdom remained unpublicised.

In order to study and follow Karma Yoga it is not adequate to refer to its literal meanings. In fact, most of the western thinkers did this and introduced wrong notions. Karma Yoga is the method of release through work, practice and activity. Karma ordains everyone to concentrate on the work. The word Karma is derived from the Sanskrit word Kri which implies to do and therefore, Karma cannot be thought of without action. Usually the word is interpreted on the effect of actions. From the metaphysical point of view, the meaning of it also includes the effects of which our actions were the causes. However, Vivekananda points out: "We have simply to do with the word Karma as meaning work. The goal of mankind is knowledge. That the one ideal placed before us by eastern philosophy. Pleasure is not the goal of man, but knowledge. Pleasure and happiness come to an end."[85] Vivekananda was the first Indian philosopher who endeavoured to infuse the civic spirit in the doctrine of Karma-Yoga. He elevated the duty to such an extent that even the belief in God is sub-ordinated to it. He observes: "Although a man has not studied a single system of philosophy, although he does not believe in any God, and never has believed, although he has not prayed even once in his whole life, if the simple power of good actions has brought him to that state where he is ready to give up his life and else for others, he has arrived at the same point to which the religious man will come through his prayers and the philosopher through his knowledge."[86] Vivekananda does not allow any option to escape from duties. He regards the Karma as the cause for the manifestation of the material and spiritual world. Thus, it is obvious that everyone should be held responsible for his present condition and his destiny is determined by his actions. Another important aspect of Karma Yoga is rejection of the theory of non-resistance to evil. Usually the followers of Indian philosophy of ancient times tend to treat non-resistance to evil as a moral ideal. In fact this was treated as a maxim to be put even into practice. In order to save the mankind from the disaster Vivekananda condemned this. He resisted this doctrine with the plea that it would ruin the social practices. In this regard Vivekananda refers to Bhagwat Gita to recall what happened at the battle field, and how the grip of despondency was loosened. Thus, it is through Gita that Vivekananda pleads the philosophy of Karma-Yoga in which non-resistance is ruled out to be a virtue. While attempting to make it clear that his stand does not contradict with the classical teachings of Hinduism, he quotes Gita: "Sri Krishna called Arjuna a coward and hypocrite, "Thou talkest like a wise man, but thy actions betray thee to be a coward; therefore, stand up and fight."[87] While suspecting the evil of non-resistance being spread by wrong interpretations, Vivekananda suggested without any concession vigorous activity and indifference to destiny of self and that of those connected to self. This makes us to believe that Vivekananda has totally deviated from the early doctrines of Hinduism where the stress was laid on renunciation. Nirvana and silencing self. Perhaps he envisages this and therefore, explained the birth of calmness through activity and said that calmness should not be considered as a synonym to inactivity. While speaking to the foreign audience, he said: "What I meant was, that a man must be active, in order to pass through activity to perfect calmness."[88]

It can be said that Vivekananda's Karma-Yoga insists on strength, activity and resistance. Perhaps, this is because of his consideration of the practical implications of the earlier theories. Having detested hypocrisy from the beginning, he appeals to all to hold activity as an ethic and important obligation.

For Vivekananda good and evil are the results reflected in our acts. Every act by nature is composed of good and evil and not a single act is an exception to this. Despite this the Karma Yoga persistently insists on activity. It is obvious from the statement: "Good and evil will both have their results, will produce their Karma. Good action will entail upon us good effect; and bad action bad. But good and bad are both bondages of the soul."[89] Vivekananda thought that if this point of view is considered as the ultimate, it may contradict the soul theory. Therefore, he refers to the teachings of Gita and advises in a typical Vedantic fashion. For a Karma Yogin, only Karma has significance. However, the ultimate goal of man or soul is the release. Since both these conditions are compulsory Vivekananda advocates that one has to work without any attachment to it. Thus attachment is the main obstacle in the path of realisation. Detachment while working is to set us free. Therefore, this kind of principle makes the soul free although the 'activity' condition is made compulsory. Lastly, it can be said that it is on the basis of this principle. Vivekananda attempts to provide guideline to emancipate self and in fact that is the crux of his Karma Yoga.

SRI AUROBINDO (1872-1950)

Sri Aurobindo's philosophy can not be confined to any particular branch of behavioural sciences or an academic discipline. It covers numerous aspects which lead us to conclude that it might have been quite sensitive to a number of direct and indirect influences. Sri Aurobindo, having studied western philosophy and literature at an impressionable age, had his 'tabula rasa' impregnated comprehensively with some of the early Greek philosophies and later particularly of Plato and Aristotle. Besides, he was also aware of the idealistic philosophies of the recent times. Therefore, the possibility of influences on him of Hegel, Whitehead, Bergson, cannot be ruled out. Nevertheless the roots of the lively tendencies that continued in his philosophical writings can be traced in the Advaita Vedanta and Yoga. He could broaden his vision and strengthen his reasoning capacity due to his intuitional knowledge and foresightedness. It is difficult to evaluate his philosophy or state with certainty that it pertains to a specific branch of philosophy as vision and intuitional knowledge can not be questioned. In a broad sense Sri Aurobindo's doctrine may be said to have based on a highly idealistic approach. At the same time with the fervour of Yoga it appears to have followed or rather preferred the isolated track of spiritualism. Sri Aurobindo conceives Reality as something spiritual and as such he visualises certain goals for the mankind. Despite this, his idealism cannot be tucked away as 'monism' of some sort. According to Haridas Choudhary: "The philosophy of Sri Aurobindo may be aptly described as integral non-dualism (Purna-advaita) or integral idealism (Purna-Vinjanana) or just integration (Purna-Vada).[90] If Sri Aurobindo's theory is accepted as non-dualistic, one is likely to think that it completely relies upon the traditional view or is based upon Advaita Vedanta. No doubt, his views are offshoots of the highly venerated Vedantic approach, particularly that of Sankara, nonetheless, they differ from the rationalistic monism which is very rigid and does not permit any scope for representing the principle of unity in any other form.

It is at this stage that he introduces the philosophy of integralism. It is generally held that reality could be determined through the arena of monism, however, Sri Aurobindo holds a different view. He neither accepts the recognized models nor points out the drawbacks of the past theories but explains the ways which lead to reality. According to him reality cannot be easily detected. For this purpose spiritual insight is necessary. His theory which is popularly known as the theory of 'Supra rational' insight well illustrates this. Nevertheless, he had to face difficulty because of the tussel between the lower nature and the higher nature or between matter and spirit. Although these subjects are poles apart, Sri Aurobindo attempts to consider the possibility of their ascendency and descendency when they function. He is one of those rare philosophers who honestly admits the contradictory nature of these and tries to sublimate through a procedural spiritual discipline. Hence in order to understand Sri Aurobindo's gigantic efforts it is necessary to examine his philosophy sectionwise. This would indicate that he dealt with various subjects and expressed his concern even for the pragmatic values.

Poorna Yoga — Integral Yoga

It is of immense importance to note that Sri Aurobindo did not attempt to lay the foundation of his school of philosophy on the basis of the usual concept of the philosopher which was then in vogue, in the West. Instead, like several philosophers in India, he also concentrated on the different levels of consciousness to find out the multiple shades of Reality. However, he could found the true meaning of the infinite power of the eternally evolving spiritual Person by going through the spell of a particular stream of consciousness. He considered thus as a sort of initial exchange which was necessary for the manifestation of the Divine grace. While he deemed it essential to unveil the barricades created by psychic phenomena. Therefore, while struggling for this purpose what appeared to Sri Aurobindo as a required discipline, has been explained in his philosophy as the instant and constant presence of the spiritual person - Purushottama - within and around. This may be called Sri Aurobindo's Yoga. Thus Yoga in this regard is not just union but 'the science of the eternal communion of the individual with the Universal self.[91] This deals with the required discipline which in turn may lead to that communion and thereby promise a great delight of the integral union. As compared to the existing Yoga schools of his time, Aurobindo has given not only a new meaning but also pointed out a path to establish on Integral Yoga. Therefore, he was more than anything a seeker for the idealised path and also a Yogi himself by all rights. Looking at his Integral Yoga one can clearly understand what this school of Yoga proposes is something exclusive. It is neither simply a set of Yogic disciplines that is proposed nor does it insist on one's own consciousness to be tagged with the Universal consciousness, but a greater responsibility is thrust upon. It asserts the collective or social salvation of all humanity, by a process of evolution. This evolution must be a conscious evolution and directed for the present as well as future. It is in this context that the usual conflict between Matter and spirit appears. These two are considered as the two Modes of same Reality, though they appear to have a stiff opposition from the beginning. In fact, such a philosophy, had been already propagated, since the advaitic times. What seems new is not just the recognition of these two but the efforts to establish a chord which is so strong that consciousness would not escape the domain of either. What had been persistently suggested demands the placement of Matter at the subsidiary level with regard to spirit. This view is even today entertained because it had been appreciated by majority of the theistic schools to show their reverence towards the spirit. Although this could also be treated as a type of Yoga only, yet for Sri Aurobindo this is not complete in itself. For him, unless matter is spiritualised totally, the true ambition of Yoga is not achieved. The descendence of the spirit is possible only if the material, vital and mental planes open themselves to receive the spiritual intensity and merges into it. Hence it can be said that as long as the gulf between these two planes is not bridged nothing is possible and the manifestation of the spirit appears to be something impossible.

It is Sri Aurobindo who expressed a novel view that soul need not escape from matter, and life and mind need not be treated as something inferior to spirit. As such his entire philosophy centres round the principle of Involution and Evolution. In this regard, creation may be considered as a movement between two involutions. That is why those involved in spirit evolve downward to the other pole of Matter. In matter too all is involved out of upwards to the other pole of spirit.[92] Therefore, it is the formless that has descended and acquired a form through two essential appearances, the Universe and the individual. These processes run counter in their directional functioning, i.e., one of them shows self-concealment while the other indicates self-revelation. They are the outcome of the Divine play. The process of concealment or revelation are steady, and gradual. Since both processes run simultaneously, a step in concealment leads to a step in revelation This is not at all a riddle, but a systematic functioning of the Divine order. Therefore, the Divine creation should be considered as real Brahman. It should not be treated as an illusion. Brahman expresses himself in various forms of consciousness through the process of transformation. Assuming material form s could be considered as the last stage of the conscious-force or 'a movement energy'. Matter represents one of such forms. Since the force is eternal it may manifest or remain unmanifested.

Materialism and Spiritualism

One of the common problems of Eastern and Western philosophers had been as to how to hold on Materialism and Spiritualism with minimum conflict. In fact, it becomes more difficult as none of them can be undermined. This does not mean that no attempts were made in the past to elevate one and denigrate the other. This could also be because of the attempts of some philosophers who wanted to generalise their personal experiences. Moreover, due to the contempt for rival theories, they did not allow their own philosophy to undergo the severe test of logic. They even did not make any attempt to openly defend it. Although these theories seem to be perfect in their claims, somehow, the traditional rivalry between them continues. Owing to this, both Materialism and Spiritualism remained poles apart and led to the emergence of two extreme views in philosophy. Surprisingly enough, both deal with the same problems concerning the world. They attempt to explain the creation of the world and the various phenomena. Very often, the rival theory is proved to be an unworthy component of its own in order to avoid any dichotomy.

Sri Aurobindo deals with this problem in an unconventional manner. He holds that due to their over-enthusiasm, these two theories claim supremacy. Nonetheless, no one independently explains all the phenomena of the world. In view of this, Aurobindo suggests an integration of these two. This philosophy of synthesis advocates deviation from the Vedic philosophical traditions in order to avoid the confrontation between them. Sri Aurobindo says: "The affirmation of a Divine life upon earth and an immortal sense in mortal existence can have no basis unless we recognize not only external spirit as the inhabitant of this bodily mansion, the wearer of this mutable robe but accept matter of which it is made, as a fit and noble material out of which He wears constantly his garbs, builds recurrently the unending series of his mansions."[93]

Thus, Sri Aurobindo believes that materialism is strong

enough as it can afford to reject spiritualism. Materialism may even go to the extent of proving that it is the only true recourse left for us and places total emphasis on it as any of the monistic doctrines would do. This kind of monism may be referred to as the monism of force or matter. Sri Aurobindo strongly believes that this monism cannot last long because it mainly takes into consideration the empirical world or the phenomenal world only. Initially it may sound convincing but later on would fizzle out when subjected to the tests of other planes which are equally necessary for human life. Everything that arises here is because of the negations. On the one hand it is the materialistic denial of the spiritual world, on the other hand, the refusal of the ascetic with regard to Matter. The former has only one postulate to rely upon and that is the sense-perception. The materialist would not accept the limitations and even scope of these sense-perceptions. The very applications look devoid of another necessary quality to be incorporated from the planes other than the physical. Since Science has strengthened the Materialism, it boasts of its scientific attitude. It is a known fact that the various properties of matter are detected and properly designated by science only. Therefore, even science may accept the subordinate position with regard to materialism. Sri Aurobindo rightly points out that even 'scientific sanction' cannot justify the materialistic denial.

Sri Aurobindo also dealt in detail the problems of materialism, on which for years together except the Lokayatas, no one paid any heed. Sri Aurobindo explains that the problems of materialism have not been satisfactorily dealt with by science. Nature unfolds certain things and conceals its secrets. Even intellect cannot overcome these limitations. At least they could formulate certain theories on the basis of assumptions and hypotheses as a possible guideline for the future. It is practically difficult to know certain reasons. Therefore, even while placing necessary stress on materialism its prospects have been automatically smothered because of overlooking 'the scientific spirit'. Scientific spirit halts at no place because it is conscious of the fact that discarding just one sheath cannot immediately lead us to the core of Reality. Even science would withdraw its support if it is made to struggle persistently for the sake of the empirical phenomena only. It totally trusts in reaching beyond the scene. Therefore, even science is not very eager to conclude something as the ultimate. The finality of a thing cannot be achieved by way of abstaining from the other possible forms in preference to something. Upon analysis, it needs to have the subject matter free from contradictions, otherwise it would itself become self-contradictory in the attempt of the denial of the non-material forms.

Coming over to the problems of the spiritualistic negation Sri Aurobindo prefers to reconsider the tendency in the religious philosophies. Therefore, he thinks that the complaints of the different schools of atheism are justified. He, therefore, declares 'spiritualistic negations' equally responsible for creating this chaos, and the unending enmity with the materialists. For him even spiritualistic negation is partial and lays unnecessarily an over emphasis on denying the materialistic claim. It believes in total rejection as clearly stated in Sankara's monism or attempts to rank low anything other than the spiritual for this cause. Since both have handed over their arguments to the formal logic, nothing seems to be resulting out of it.

One of the root causes inferred by Sri Aurobindo for this state had been the typical ascetic mentality which claims the knowledge of the super-sensible realities. The ascetics also feel that theirs could be the only route for gaining such a knowledge and nothing can distract them. Similarly they also think that senses do provide knowledge but that is not to be taken as the only necessary medium. In fact, they also think that they can do away with it and yet whatever they capture would prove a sort of ratified knowledge likely to remain unattainable for others. In view of Sri Aurobindo, this very thought leads its followers to conclude that the domain of reality is under the control of spiritual world only. They go to the level of denying the reality of the materialistic world. Therefore, the very birth of 'Illusion-Brahma' or can be rightly translated as the 'cosmic illusion' takes place for the ascetics. They straightway overlook a simple underlying fact in their enthusiasm or because of being one-sided.

Sri Aurobindo opines: 'If reality is spiritual then even matter is spiritual and therefore, its outright rejection is fallacious.'[94]

The latest trend in science overlooks the traditionally drawn line of demarcation between matter and energy, with the presumption that even matter is a stationary form of energy. Therefore, everything around us is nothing but a sheer representation of energy in various forms due to transformations. These forms are interconvertible and that is the sole reason as to why energy gets conserved but not destroyed. However, it is a practice with us to refer to the stagnated form of energy as something different from it. Change in the phase or state immediately brings to our mind, loss of energy, which is totally incorrect. Sri Aurobindo has a similar view point while describing the concepts of matter and energy. He considers them as the two aspects of the same thing. He, therefore, believes in the possible synthesis of both in the light of the ascendency of matter and the descendency of spirit. This is the reason as to why in Sri Aurobindo's philosophy spirit does not enjoy the isolated status given by the ancient and mediaeval philosophers. However, he cautions that unless both the processes operate simultaneously, the operative synthesis as proposed by him is impossible. Therefore, the usual method of discarding matter in preference to spirit must be corrected. With this, both matter and spirit can have an independent placement or status in connection with the reality.

To sum it Sri Aurobindo remains very critical about the age old Vedantic approach. Therefore, in his critique of pure forms of materialism and Spiritualism he prefers to introduce the two important terms Evolution and Involutions. He thinks that one of the grave mistakes committed by Vedanta is that it does not realise that every evolution must have a corresponding involution. This view prompts us to take up an integral view in which both matter and spirit are not only duly recognized as independent entities but also their involvement in shaping the process leading to Reality.

S.K.Moitra tries to make the whole idea clear with the help of a very apt analogy when he says: "The usual view of evolution, which looks upon it as a mere ascent from the lower grade, may be compared to the march of an army which advances without keeping its line of communication with the base intact. And, we may compare Sri Aurobindo's concept of evolution with the march of an army which advances with the whole force, keeping all its lines of communication perfectly intact."[95]

Ignorance: Origin and Nature

Sri Aurobindo's metaphysics clearly indicates that the concept of ignorance deserves an important place. It is not unusual to find in the Indian philosophical traditions that the entire world is conceived as being the realm of ignorance and evolution is conceived as gradual progression from ignorance to knowledge. Therefore, it is necessary to attempt to know the nature of ignorance. On analysis, it will be seen that majority of the Indian philosophers prefer to relate ignorance to Maya, which according to them is the power of the reality to produce cosmic illusion. Further, ignorance is also believed to be the antithesis of knowledge and a sure cause of suffering. The only aim of spiritual activity is, therefore, to deliver man free from it.

Sri Aurobindo partially subscribes to this common view. He believes that evolution is the evolution from ignorance towards knowledge. However, he does not accept that ignorance is absence of knowledge. According to him both knowledge and ignorance are fundamentally similar in nature and there is no reason to emphasize the opposition between the two. He also feels that once the integral character of knowledge is accepted the concept of ignorance as opposed to knowledge will create logical difficulties. Sri Aurobindo traces the source of this concept in Rgveda, where knowledge signifies consciousness of the truth while ignorance as unconsciousness of the truth. Therefore, the Vedantists upheld this idea and highlighted the antinomy. It is in this context that Sri Aurobindo feels that the Vedantic thinkers have caused a greater damage than any by creating a permanent gap between the two. Therefore, he conceives ignorance also a form of knowledge and insists it to be treated as atleast a partial or fragmentary type. At its best it may remain as the extreme state of complete nescience. The other extreme end is the state of complete knowledge. In between these two lies the state of ignorance.

The problem regarding the origin of Ignorance has remained for long quite puzzling for the entire tradition of Indian philosophy. Sri Aurobindo's solution to this problem, may seem to be similar to that of the Vedantic solution, but in reality it differs significantly. The Vedantists consider mind, which is the seat of ignorance, is a part or reflection of illusion. Therefore, even ignorance becomes an illusion. Some of the Vedantists refer to this as cosmic illusion. For some of the Vedantists it is only the absolute which is free from ignorance whereas the individual is attached to ignorance. For Sri Aurobindo none of these concepts are agreeable regarding the origin of ignorance. He feels that any solution which engenders the integral unity of a reality is not at all impossible. Regarding Ignorance, he says: "Ignorance must be part of the movement of the one, a development of its consciousness knowingly adopted, to which it is not forcibly subjected but which it uses for its cosmic purpose."[96]

To follow Sri Aurobindo's argument stepwise analysis is a must. Since ignorance is understood as a stage in the development of the process of knowledge, the answer for the difficulty in tracing the origin of ignorance should be searched only in the dynamic form of the consciousness. This is because the Divine consciousness is always understood as a force. When closely examined, this force which Sri Aurobindo calls-Tapas-is resolved into two aspects. They are, the active aspect and the passive aspect. The former results through actions, internal or external, but the latter either produces no action or at the most mechanical acts which are automatic actions, performed unconsciously. Just parallel to this even the Divine consciousness must have been composed of the two aspects. The active aspect is responsible for the creation while the passive aspect has nothing to do with the activities on the surface. However, the passive aspect is in large excess. Sri Aurobindo makes it clear with the help of the analogy of ocean and its waves in which waves are the active aspects of the ocean. The two are not separate. They represent the same energy or force.

The attempt to determine the nature of knowledge calls for an explanation of the various forms of aspects of ignorance. The reason already stated is that ignorance does not necessarily mean absence of knowledge but rather incomplete or partial knowledge and also because it is from the state of ignorance that one has to grow into the state of knowledge. As basically ignorance is the very state of our separative existence, and therefore, in order to determine the various aspects and modes of ignorance we have to realize the state of our ordinary existence. Sri Aurobindo opines that such an examination or analysis will at once indicate that," ...... this ignorance in which ordinarily we live by the very circumstance of our separative existence in a material, in a spatial and temporal universe, we see that on its obscurer side it reduces itself, from whatever direction we look at or approach, into the fact of a many sided self-ignorance."[97] It is in this light only that he recommends the sevenfold aspects of self-ignorance. They are the original ignorance, the cosmic ignorance, the egoistic ignorance, the temporal ignorance, the psychological ignorance, the Constitutional ignorance and the practical ignorance.

These seven sides of the self-ignorance have been explained by Sri Aurobindo in detail to show how each can encompass certain region of consciousness. Each has its own capacity to halt the movement of consciousness which is striving to get released from the sevenfold ignorance. It is quite customary to infer the nature of the things around us as they seem to us. This creates the original ignorance because we take the things for granted as they first appealed to us. Since this ignorance has proved to be the true cause of the other types of ignorance mentioned, it is designated as 'Original Ignorance'. This also promotes our ideas regarding the Absolute and the nature of the cosmos. The world in which we live and sense the objects within it are taken for granted by us. Therefore, the world of space and time is thought as real and the changes which occur in it also appear to be real. This according to Sri Aurobindo is the ignorance of the universe itself and therefore, should be called 'The Cosmic Ignorance'. Further as if the chain of ignorance continues, Sri Aurobindo suggests that somehow one feels that it is the embodied individual that represents the real self. This is what contributes to the Egoistic Ignorance. In Sri Aurobindo's own words," ...... We take our limited egoistic mentality, vitality, corporeality for our true self and regard everything other than that as not self."[98] It is also to be confessed that we are ignorant of our eternal nature also. Probably this is the reason as to why we believe that our life span represents the essence of existence. This is why we take every part of space and time as vital aspects of ourself. It is at this juncture that we fail to understand that our true nature is somehow beyond these spatial or temporal dimensions. As this ignorance is the result of the temporal conditions around us, it is called the temporal ignorance. Another closely related ignorance is the Psychological Ignorance which develops due to the sense of experience to which we give maximum importance. Sri Aurobindo feels that normally we take the superficial aspects of our life and behaviour as constituting the real aspects of ourself. In fact, we fail to understand that this is an extremely negligible and superficial aspect of our existence. There are indeed deeper regions of our being which do not fall into this trap, but truly constitute our real nature. As we ignore the super conscient, the sub-conscient, the intraconscient and the circum-conscient, the psychological ignorance dominates the scene. Another ignorance which for us unknowingly contributes is the constitutional ignorance. It is deep rooted and resides in our constitution of normal existence. This is because we often think that it is the group comprising of our mind, body and energy, that represents our constitution. This is of course a very common view carried by us. In this impression we do not pay attention to the deeper aspects of our constitution. In fact, it is these aspects which build, nourish and sustain, the activities of different planes. Similarly, as all these types of Ignorance contribute sectionally, on the whole we mismanage our practical life, which further results into the practical ignorance. It is this Ignorance which makes the life chaotic and even aimless. It is also due to desperation that we mess up everything. Sri Aurobindo describes this very systematically. "As a result of all these ignorances (the first six) we miss the true knowledge, government and enjoyment of our life in the world; we are ignorant in our thought, will, sensations, actions, return wrong or imperfect response at every point to the questioning of the world, wander in a maze of errors and desires, strivings and failures, pain and pleasure, sin and stumbling follow a crooked road, grope blindly for a changing goal, that is the seventh, the practical Ignorance."[99]

The Theory of Supermind

Sri Aurobindo having accepted the different forms and necessary stage of Reality suggests a division in the realm of the Reality. There are two recognised hemispheres, viz., the higher, and the lower, to erect the Reality in its complete form. The higher hemisphere is represented by the triune principle-Saccidananda - i.e., Existence, Consciousness and Bliss. The lower hemisphere has matter, life, psyche and mind. Sri Aurobindo expects the evolution to reach the state of mind and now it is from this stage that a preparation for a higher stage is expected. It is always a sort of leap, which could fill the gap between the lower hemisphere and the higher hemisphere. Therefore, a principle to govern this leap is necessary. The principle, no doubt, must have its roots in the lower hemisphere but should also have been directed towards the higher hemisphere. This indicates that Sri Aurobindo expects no opposition between the mental and the governing principle. Similarly, in essence, the principle has to coincide with the nature of the triune principle - Sacchidananda. In his spiritual aspiration, Sri Aurobindo desires a strong link between the two hemispheres. This link is called the Supermind. Although the supermind belongs to the higher hemisphere, yet it remains as an idealized aim to the mind. Therefore, as Sri Aurobindo suggests, it is necessary to understand here that mind and Supermind belong to he same spirit but mind is stationed at the point of inception while the Supermind is thoroughly attuned to the higher hemisphere. In other words, the Supermind is totally aligned with the principle of Saccidanda and is the culmination of mind. Sri Aurobindo often refers to the Supermind as the creator, the Real Idea, the supreme-truth consciousness. Similarly, he wants to differentiate between the mind and Supermind on the basis of the difference between their manner of apprehending reality. Supermind essentially grasps the unitary picture of reality while the mind can catch only the bits. Therefore, it is the mind that creates divisions. Therefore, realising the capacity of the Supermind and having an urge for the same become the major characteristic of the mind. That is why it strives to catch the supramental level. Basant Kumar Lal describes this as "That is why Sri Aurobindo says that mind is actually a fall from Supermind. This fall, according to him, is a necessary condition of creation, because it represents the descent of the spirit. That makes it a precondition of evolution also. If supermind is not there already concealed-hidden-or inside a veil, how can mind hope to ascend to the supramental level. And, it is because supermind is already-potentially there in mind that it aspires to ascend to the supermind."[100]

As we can see at no place a change from one extreme to the other extreme can be abrupt. There has to be a transition state wherein the subject has neither any connection to the initial state nor to the final state. It is the position at which the subject is successful in detaching itself from its earlier bondage and can only aspire for the new relation. Sri Aurobindo has shown the different intermediary steps through which this change can be brought about. They are to begin with the mind, higher mind, Illumined Mind, Intuition Overmind and then the Supermind. This journey is from Nature to Super Nature or Mental to Supermental or Mind to Supermind.

The starting point, i.e., Mind is also consciousness, with a tendency to gauge the indivisible wholes but in a fragmentary fashion. Therefore, it treats parts of the whole as separate elements. This is where it lacks the maturity of thought, and contemplation. Owing to this it fails to grasp the true nature of the reality, and therefore, it is desired that it should cultivate some capacity through certain modes.

The very primary condition for this is that the mind must prepare itself to know its capacities or limitations and exercise some control over them. When the mind emerges through this, then it becomes higher mind. The higher mind represents the parent nucleus of the mental ideation. This is a state where the usual activities of the mind come to a halt or there is no longer any need of a ratiocination. This also means that the usual reasoning, logic or inference lose their importance. The mind escapes from the realm of ignorance to make a sensible entry into the world of the ideal.

Sri Aurobindo thinks that even this higher mind is not free from the empirical and rational pressure. It cannot have true knowledge of the ultimate at this rung of the consciousness. The light within cannot shine perfectly so as to have an insight faultlessly. The spiritual light which illuminates continuously cannot have its full range to be effective. Therefore, what is required is an Illumined Mind. The qualities of the Illumined Mind are quite exclusive because it proceeds always by vision and not just by thought. Thought process is not exactly debased in comparison with the vision but is certainly subordinated in order to facilitate the latter to provide a deep insight. Sri Aurobindo says, "A consciousness that proceeds by sight, the consciousness of seer, is a greater power of knowledge than the consciousness of the thinker. The perpetual power of the inner sight is greater and more direct than the perpetual power of thought ... As the higher mind brings a greater consciousness into the being through the spiritual idea and its power of truth, so the Illumined Mind brings in a still greater consciousness through a true-sight and truth-light and its seeing and seizing power."[101]

Despite the fact that these two levels speak of a very high state in the path of evolution, yet Sri Aurobindo is of the opinion that unless we allow the intuition within to supplement these two, nothing can be fulfilled truly and the consciousness may not have all its power at stake. Thus, what is normally thought about intuition is not recognised by Sri Aurobindo. Usually intuition is viewed as an unreasonable flight of mind and whenever it coincides with reality it is thought as a chance. With the rational analysis, intuition may not find any proper placement. On the other hand, intuition is conceived as a power of consciousness nearer and highly intimate to knowledge than any of the two previous stages. The usual danger, however, remains as it is. This may even lead to a wrong notion, whenever differentiating between true intuition and consciousness free intuition becomes impossible. Therefore, Sri Aurobindo has laid down the condition that unless the consciousness of the subject meets the consciousness residing in the object, it cannot be the intuition desired. It is at this stage that consciousness really vibrates due to its perfect contact. Sri Aurobindo describing the nature of intuition says, "Intuition has a fourfold power, a power of revelatory truth-seeing, a power of inspiration or truth-hearing, a power of truth-touch or immediate seizing of significance... (and) a power of true and automatic discrimination of the orderly and exact relation of truth to truth."[102]

This is how Sri Aurobindo constitutes the power of Intuition. He does not allow the only possible metaphysical element to dominate so as to have most of its reflection seem highly wishful. It is also indicated through this fourfold principle that Intuition in its rightly suggested form can be really near the truth. Sri Aurobindo also trusts that intuition can play the roles of reason and also intelligence. Therefore, Intuition can prove fruitful in the process of 'Integration'. In fact, according to Sri Aurobindo's philosophy, Intuition is the starting point for the process. This itself shows that Intuition may trigger the process but cannot catalyse, the same to accelerate it, so as to bring about the completion. Therefore, complete integration does demand some more conditions. The highest form of consciousness cannot be rightly erected just on the dint of Intuition. One of the major difficulties which it has to face is the intereference caused by the mental faculties. Pure intuition is easily marked by reason and intelligence. The second difficulty that arises out of Intuition itself is because of its remaining very short lived. Yet another difficulty could be due to its expression which has to permeate through the worldly medium of immediate reasoning and therefore, it might not be 'properly expressed'.

It is necessary that Intuition overcomes these obstacles as to develop into another faculty, recommended by Sri Aurobindo. This new faculty is called the Overmind. This Overmind is in direct contact with the Supermind which is the ultimate in consciousness. Therefore, the Overmind is doubly made up due to its being at the helm of the cosmic consciousness and also in tune with the Supermind. The former stages viz., Mind, Higher Mind, Illumined Mind, Intuition, also have, to their lot, certain portion of the consciousness but at this stage, i.e., the Overmind, the consciousness itself widens fully due to the pattern of ascendency. The knowledge becomes global. It is in this regard that the earlier stages even with their limitations look meaningful. Speaking about the qualities of the Overmind, Sri Aurobindo points out: "The Overmind... is the final consummating movement of the dynamic spiritual transformation, it is the highest possible status-dynamis of the spiritual - mind plane. It takes up all that is in the three steps below in and raises their characteristic workings to their highest and largest power adding to them a universal wideness of consciousness and force, a harmonious concert of knowledge, a more manifold delight of being."[103]

What has been ascribed to the Overmind by Sri Aurobindo is mainly by taking into account the close vicinity in which the Overmind is residing with the Supermind. Therefore, every action is perfectly spiritualised by the flash of light received from the Supermind which is Sacchidananda - an embodiment of the triune principle. Although the Overmind has a direct rapport with the Supermind, yet the Overmind is not same as the Supermind. The Overmind does not have the integral character of the Supermind. The latter can have a thorough view of the reality apprehending the supreme truth as a unity. Overmind does not possess this power. The difference between these two is clearly stated by Sri Aurobindo as:

"It (Overmind) is a power... the highest power of the lower hemisphere; although its basis is a cosmic unity, its action is an action of division and inter-action, an action taking its stand on the play of the multiplicity. Its play is, like that of all mind, a play of possibilities; although it acts not in ignorance but with the knowledge of the truth of these possibilities, yet it works them out through their own independent evolution of their powers."[104]

Therefore, in the Overmind the integral view is not found. This could be possible if the membrane separating the two hemispheres is erased. Such a change is possible only on a cosmic level. As it is pointed out: "A supramental change... takes place when the involved supermind in Nature emerges to meet and join the supermental light and power descending from supernature."[105]

NOTES AND REFERENCES

1. S. Radhakrishnan, Indian Philosophy, Vol. I, p. 8,
2. P.T. Raju, The Philosophical Traditions of India, pp. 14-15.
3. *Ibid.*, p. 327.
4. B.G. Tilak, Gita Rahasya, Third Edition, p.273.
5. Mahadevan and Saroja, Contemporary Indian Philosophy, p. 74.
6. *Ibid.*
7. H. Rashadall, The Theory of Good and Evil, Vol. II, p. 434
8. *Ibid.*, p.75.
9. *Ibid.*, p.76.
10. Charles Landesman, Philosophy - An introduction to the Centrals Issues, pp. 43-44.
11. Kant, Fundamental Principles of the Metaphysics of Morals - translated by Thomas K. Abbott, p. 35.
12. *Ibid.*, pp. 35-36.
13. *Ibid.*, p. 38.
14. H. J. Paton, The Moral Law, p. 56.
15. Gita Rahasya, op. cit., p. 247.
16. Ct. in 'Tilak's Metaphysic of Morals', B.R. Kulkarni, p.6.
17. Vedantasara - Ed. H. Hirianna, p. 365.
18. Gitarahsya - op. cit., p. 129.
19. *Ibid.*, p. 132.
20. J. S. Mill, Utilitarianism, p. 6.
21. Gitarahasya, op. cit. p. 132.
22. Mahadevan and Saroja, Contemporary Indian Philosophy, p. 76.
23. Gitarahasya, op. cit., p. 127.
24. *Ibid.*, p. 685.
25. Quoted in Lokmanya Tilak's Metaphysics of Morals, B. R. Kulkarni, p. 22.
26. D. S. Sarma, Lectures and Essays on the Bhagwad Gita, p. 36.
27. Gitarahasya, op. cit., pp. 373-374.
28. *Ibid.*, p. 374.
29. Lokmanya Tilak's Metaphysic of Morals, B. R. Kulkarni, p. 25.
30. R. D. Ranade, The Bhagwat Gita is a Philosophy of God, Realisation, p. 207.
31. B. R. Kulkarni, Lokmanya Tilak's Metaphysic of Marks, p. 31.
32. Kant, Critique of Practical Reason, Trans, by T. K. Abbott - p. 55.
33. Rabindranath Tagore, 'Stray Birds', p. 130.
34. Tagore, 'Sadhana'.

35. Tagore, Gitanjali, Poem 73, MacMillan, 1938.
36. Tagore, The Religion of Man, p. 107.
37. Tagore, 'Sadhana', p. viii.
38. 'Rabindranath as a Vedantist', Visvā Bharati, Quarterly, May/October, 1941.
39. Radhakrishnan, 'The Philosophy of Rabindranath', p. vii.
40. Tagore, The Religion of Man, p. 57.
41. V. S. Narvane, An Introduction to R. Tagore, p. 26.
42. Lectures and Addresses of Rabindranath Tagore, Ed. by Anthony Sons, p. 146.
43. Tagore, Sadhana, p. 41.
44. Tagore, Gitanjali, Poem No. 147.
45. Tagore, Gitanjali, Poem No. 63.
46. B. K. Lal, Contemporary Indian Philosophy, p. 51.
47. Tagore, The Religion of Man, p. 114.
48. *Ibid.*, p. 130.
49. Tagore, Personality, p. 44.
50. Tagore, The Kind of the Dark Chamber, p. 9.
51. Tagore, Creative Unity, p. 35.
52. Ct. in the Philosophy of R. Tagore, by S. Radhakrishnan, p. 70.
53. Tagore, The Religion of Man, p. 228.
54. Tagore, Lover's Gift and Crossing, 'Crossing', p. 30.
55. Tagore, Gitanjali, Poem No. 54.
56. Tagore, Sadhana, p. 48.
57. *Ibid.*, p. 52.
58. *Ibid.*, pp. 66-67.
59. Janamadine, quoted in R. T. by G. R. Ray, p. 341, Indian Thought, Ed. by D. Bishop.
60. Tagore, Gitanjali, Poem No. 35.
61. Quoted in Contemporary thought of India, p. 175, A. C. Underwood.
62. *Ibid.*,
63. V. S. Narvane, The Philosophy of Rabindranath Tagore, p. 27.
64. Mahadevan and Saroja, Contemporary Indian Philosophy, pp. 102-103.
65. V. S. Narvane, The Philosophy of Tagore, p. 30.
66. *Ibid.*, p. 28.
67. *Ibid.*, p. 32.
68. V. S. Narvane, Modern Indian Thought, p. 60.
69. The Complete Works of Vivekananda, Vol. III, p. 324.
70. *Ibid.*, p. 323.
71. Vivekananda, The Complete Works, Vol. V., p. 323.
72. Vivekananda, The Complete Works, Vol. VIII, p. 246.

73. Ct. Indian Philosophy in Modern Times, V. Bordor, p. 216.
74. Vivekananda, Jnana Yoga, pp. 119-120.
75. B. K. Lal, Contemporary Indian Philosophy, p. 16.
76. Thomas Mann, The Living Thoughts of Schopenhauer, p. 4.
77. *Ibid.*, p. 34.
78. V. Brodor, Indian Philosophy in Modern Times.
79. Thomas Mann, The Living Thoughts of Schopenhauer, p. 69.
80. Swami Vivekananda's Works, Vol. VI p. 22, (Ed. 89).
81. Swami Vivekananda's Works, Vol. 2, p. 234, (1989. Ed.).
82. Swami Vivekananda, Jnana Yoga, p. 278.
83. Vivekananda, The Complete Works, Vol. VIII, p. 249.
84. Vivekananda, Jnana Yoga, p. 394.
85. Complete Works of Vivekananda, Vol. I, p. 27 (Ed. 1889).
86. Complete Works of Vivekananda, Vol. I, p. 84 (Ed. 1955).
87. Complete works, Vol. I, p. 37 (Ed. 1955).
88. *Ibid.*, p. 38.
89. *Ibid.*, p. 51.
90. Haridas Choudhary, The Integral Philosophy of Sri Aurobindo, p. 19.
91. R. R. Diwakar, Sri Aurobindo, p. 329.
92. Sri Aurobindo, Sri Aurobindo Birth Centenary Library, Sri Aurobindo Ashram, Pondicherry, India, 1972, Vol. 18, p. 129.
93. Life Divine, p.8.
94. *Ibid.*
95. S. K. Moitra, The Philosophy of Sri Aurobindo, pp. 64-67.
96. Life Divine, p. 506.
97. Life Divine, p. 583.
98. *Ibid.*
99. Life Divine, p. 584.
100. B. K. Lal, Contemporary Indian Philosophy, p. 198.
101. Life Divine, p. 839.
102. *Ibid.* , p. 843.
103. *Ibid.*, p. 846.
104. *Ibid.*, p. 846.
105. *Ibid.*, p. 855.

[illegible]

[illegible] Sri Aurobindo, Birth Centenary Library, [illegible]
Ashram, Pondicherry, India, 1972, Vol. 18, p. [illegible]

[illegible] S. K. Maitra, The Philosophy of Sri Aurobindo, pp. [illegible]
The Life Divine, p. [illegible]

[illegible] Life Divine, p. [illegible]
[illegible] Contemporary Indian Philosophy, p. [illegible]
[illegible] Life Divine, p. [illegible]
[illegible] Ibid., p. [illegible]
[illegible] Ibid., p. [illegible]
[illegible] Ibid., p. [illegible]

4

Conclusion

Having examined various aspects of tradition and modernity in the preceding chapters, it can be said that the study of contemporary philosophers needs exploration of the movements or events in the past which inspired them. Therefore, the indifference towards the past in the enthusiasm to accept modernity is likely to lead to confusion. Similarly, it is also necessary to scrutinise certain selective philosophical traditions as they help us to understand the different points of view. Otherwise, all our efforts to link the traditions of various cultures would prove to be a mere formality. By and large, the Indian philosophers seem to have focussed their attention to find out the truth. This is obvious from the fact, they discovered various shades of truth and frankly acknowledged them. There is no point in passing on sharp criticism about the judgements of the counterparts in the west. Philosophy is not a monopoly of any country or culture. The strength of argument lies in providing new aspects but not in contradicting others' inferences. Similarly highlighting one's own problem as a genuine one does not build any status. Any ism for that matter must be exposed to the metaphysical and cultural interpretation before recognizing it as an important or significant addition to the already existing group of isms.

Needless to say, philosophers think and therefore, they voluntarily suffer. It is these sufferings which enable them to reset their thinking pattern and therefore, they are in a position to throw light on new aspects. Besides, Indian philosophy experienced great social and political upheavals because it had foreign rulers for centuries. They not only intervened in the country's freedom but also in the cultural premises. Therefore, Indian philosophy can boast of different experiences which may now fancy the onlookers. Surely it is the rich cultural heritage that has always come to rescue when upsets were at large. Under such trying circumstances it is indeed praiseworthy that the Indian contemporary philosophers could excel wonderfully. At the same time it cannot be denied that working for the universal problems in philosophy may have brought in at certain stages cultural crosss fertilization. This has been confessed but it has served a better purpose. Now it may be commented that for some time the Indians found the need of examining own culture and heritage, with alien people. Naturally, this was not a pleasant experience. However, this practice did not last long and the credit goes to the contemporary Indian philosophers. To summarise the kinds of influence quoting Ainslie Embree would be worthwhile.

"One reaction was indifference, and this was not purely negative in its results, for it meant that religious and social movements that had their roots in the Hindu tradition continued to flourish, and the nineteenth century saw a remarkable proliferation of cults and sects of all kinds with Hinduism. But even though these movements seem completely indigenous in their inspiration, it is quite possible that they were reflecting a general malaise caused by the intrusion of the West...... Another, and very different response, was the rejection of the old tradition and the acceptance of everything Western, including Christianity. This attitude was not very common, but it is contributed to the general process of growth and change that characterized the time. More common, and of much greater significance, was the reaction to the West that was both critical and selective. Aware of the weakness within traditional Hindu society, many sought to reform it by using features of western culture...... This classification covers a wide spectrum of opinion, including individuals of the most antithetical views such as Rammohan Roy, K.C. Sen, the Tagore family, Vivekananda, Aurobindo Ghosh, Gokhale, Ranade, and Gandhi. The fourth reaction was outright and hostile rejection of the values and ideas of the Western world...... but here again the range of opinion, and degree of rejection, varied greatly."[1] Thus during the last and present centuries, much of the exchange took place between the West and East. The traditions belonged to different fields. As time rolled on Hinduism also responded to the incoming flow of cultural influences.

It must be borne in mind that there are various problems which are beyond the purview of this study. on tradition and change. This shows how rich the field of philosophical investigation and classical Indian thought is. The outstanding problems which are likely to crop up in future are related to Indian philosophical traditions, yet they can be matter of concern for any philosopher. To begin with, the unfortunate part of the Indian philosophical thinking is that it frequently entertains the attitude that only Indian classical thought is merely interesting as a historic phenomenon. Therefore, what is needed is philosophers who are willing to push the old way of thinking but within the extensible limits. The future philosophers must work on the traditional lines before justifying or refuting them. At any rate they should not be looked upon as dead ideas. This is a primary condition to develop the new currents in Indian philosophy. In case this is ignored we may end up with the numerous missing links and our position will be quite deplorable.

There are many exciting avenues of philosophical analysis and construction that deserve our attention. They present challenges from the very nature of classical Indian thought. We have already the logical conclusions drawn by the contemporary philosophers, yet there is sufficient scope to explore. One of the problems is regarding the ethical and scientific reasonings. Ethical reasoning though based on the need of the time, can survive only if backed by a set of rigorous moral principles. Similarly, most of the times, scientific reasoning has only empirical experiences to its credit, which are certainly inadequate. Philosophers who would attempt this difficult task of verification of either form of reasoning would be really doing a service. With regard to scientific reasoning any discussion we might enter into, must remain necessarily tentative and suggestive only. This is due to the fact that the new discoveries may change the whole argument. Therefore, the interpretations will have a different frame of reference. Though philosophical traditions need not take into account the technical developments, in the strict academic sense, yet they are concerned because such developments have a close bearing on civilization.

Besides, in view of the present need, the distinction between analytic and synthetic, between a priori and a posteriori, between formal and inductive logic has to be carried out on definite grounds. This is likely to remain a demand of few more decades. Karl H. Potter opines: "The Indians did not find the distinctions relevant. Might it not be that we have worked ourselves into a cul-de-sac on this issue, drawn there under the domination of the scholastic and Aristotelian tradition which in other respects we have come to reject?"[2] At present whether in West or East there are only two kinds of philosophers drawing our attention. They are the progress philosophers and the Leap philosophers. These philosophers have emerged due to the upholding of the independent nature of philosophy which actually demands openness and attention directed towards the progressive tendency. According to them, in the past the concept of philosophy was quite cumbersome and therefore, instead of clarification of issues, much delight was taken in discovering new issues. Therefore, the progress and leap philosophers suggest that the efforts should be made to lay bare man's true nature by encouraging doubts rather than discouraging them. As far as the Indian philosophical traditions are concerned, attempts have been made to create awareness which was considered as the major function of philosophy. Even then, "Progress philosophers in India have searched for a dependence relation as a model for causation. Is this not what Western philosophers have frequently been doing, too? Why the continuing dissatisfaction with the Human account of causation, for instance, as well as with the alternative account along the lines of logical necessity? Are not the aims of both Indian and Western philosophy very similar at this point? If so, a consideration of the details of the Indians' investigations of the problems surrounding dependence relations should shed light on our concerns."[3]

The investigations reveal that somehow the intrinsic problems even if pushed aside forcefully, may make a reappearance in some form or the other. A single reference would suffice to substantiate this point. For example, Aryans brought Vedic culture to this country and made it compulsory for all. Before their arrival whatever ideas might have existed, but we do not find any resistance from them to the Aryan ideals. Later on when the unorthodox or heterodox schools openly began to oppose the validity of the authority of Vedas, they were almost discarded or assigned a subsidiary position. However, it was the job of the philosophers to highlight the true contribution made by these schools. In fact they renewed the faith by directly attacking the non-sensical parts. They also showed it to the Western world that the claims of the ancient Indian philosophers and their followers were not without qualifications. One such example may be cited here, "Philosophically speaking, this conception of everything having its being only in an eternal flux was by far the most significant contribution of early Buddhism and it is not a little surprising to note that precisely the same view along with the same illustration of fire, was proclaimed about a generations later by Heraclitus in ancient Greece and, further, is being reinstated, though of course with an incomparably richer content, by modern science."[4] This shows that what Heraclitus did for early Greek philosophy was also done by the Buddhists for early Indian philosophy. For this reason if the approach is considered scientific on the part of the Buddhists then it would be faulty because it was rather a religious reaction than establishing scientific temperament or thinking. This throws a greater responsibility and challenge to the forth-coming philosophical traditions.

Science which attempts to know the true picture of the Universe ends up its search with the collection of the empirical facts and has to halt because the secrets of Nature have always been hidden from our physically limited senses. It is self-evident that our conscious awareness is only subjected to illusion of the senses but to the delusions of mind as well. In order to compensate this we have taken interest in erecting systems out of logic and the so called rational methods are adopted to judge the functioning of the world or rhythm of Nature. In the process one of the philosophically acknowledged methods of gaining knowledge, viz., Imagination or Intuition is proved to be outdated. However it may satisfy those thinkers who opt to believe only in the discursive reasoning method. The sufferer on the whole will be the common man as he wants to be neither a scientist nor a philosopher. Even then he needs the true knowledge of the world which includes empirical knowledge, and also the one based on the experiences of the evolved beings who possess far stretched insight. His concern for the basic amenities is easily outweighed by the metaphysical enquiries because he can manage the former. Therefore, the problems of Reality, Evil, Life, Death, Rebirth, Soul and so many allied to them really disturb him. As the eminent physicist Max Planck wrote in his Autobiography: "When the pioneer in science sends forth the groping fingers of his thoughts, he must have a vivid, intuitive imagination, for new ideas are not generated by deductive, but by and artistically creative imagination."[5] The scientist who wants in a mechanised environment does not entirely exclude human error because despite the gain in data the interpretation is his own. In short, unless a new dimension in philosophy as well as science is introduced with an intention of welcoming the rival, none of these subjects can truly improve or do something worthwhile. Philosophers on their part have to admit the necessity of scientific thinking to sharpen their vision. While science in turn must look to philosophy as a lodestar.

Another important issue had been the problem of synthesis. We have in our contemporary philosophers the urge to synthesize matter and spirit and they have been successful in doing so. For example Sri Aurobindo asserts for the Integral philosophy which makes matter and spirit quite clear. His philosophy also guides everyone who seeks the path of realization. Tagore's contention strengthens confidence in humanity as he pleads for the existence of a strong bond between humanity and divinity. Tilak has explained the philosophical principles of Gita and their implications to make every individual realise the worth of liberation of the self. Swami Vivekananda almost rearranged the limbs of Yoga to suit the necessities of the modern mind. Ramkrishna toiled to preserve Indian philosophical wealth and he retaliated all the Christian criticism in general. We had K.C. Bhattacharya serving purely academic philosophy and Sir Mohammed Iqbal who proposed resurrection of man. Nevertheless it appears that there is hardly a class of philosophers which is keen on bridging the gulf between East and West. No doubt, some of our writings stem out of the Western philosophical standpoints or isms and carry the influence stealthily to escape any criticism. This is indeed a sorry state because though Western and Eastern writers, thinkers and philosophers have mutual appreciation there are no endeavours to coagulate the theories or philosophies to gain universalization. This would be a task before the philosophy because unless it is provided the complete horizon of the world may have to remain with definite and limited idealism to serve partially the humanity.

The next problem to be combated is the problem of representation. It is quite disheartening to see that Indian philosophy is often referred to as synonymous to Hinduism or to the religions pertaining to Hindus. Though in minority, there have been many extant religions which really contribute to Indian philosophy or some of them do not intervene with it. Buddhism, Jainism and Islamic philosophies but for their different basic postulates match with the spirit of the Hindu philosophy. We have in Iqbal's philosophy problems like Nature of Intuition, Nature of the self, Nature of the world, Space and Time, concept of God, Proofs for the existence of God, Human Destiny and Importance of Prayer. Needless to say Buddha and Jaina suggested corrective measures and rightly exposed the superificiality of ritualism and pretence that had not just gathered but started dominating the scene. There are various proofs in print to show that Buddhism and Jainism are the branches of Hinduism only and therefore, they should not be treated as aliens.

Moreover, Indian philosophy despite its accommodative nature does not quickly respond to the new tendencies developing in its field, particularly from the West. It has become partly customary for the Indian Philosophers to remain indifferent to the recent waves and that is why they always sound rigid or unreasonably complacent. Another reasoning put forward by them is that having known and accepted the Ultimate, it is wise only to exert for the realization than waste time in further investigations. This attitude is not so philosophical when we are concerned with the academic discipline of the subject. We have been in the habit of mixing the issues of spirituality with philosophical endeavours, though it is undeniable that at certain stages they do form an admixture with each other. However, this practice may leave us only to be content with our past achievements and enjoy the nostalgia thereof to substantiate this it can be said that we cannot mention a few names who have contributed sufficiently in the last and present centuries to existentialism. Positivism, Agnosticism, Pragmatism and Formalism. No doubt our philosophers have given passing references to these in their writings. Of course it is necessary to mention that some of the isms had been short-lived. Even then we are still facing the difficulty when we have to reckon some names for exclusive contribution to any of the branches of philosophy. This is the need of the time and challenge for the contemporary Indian philosophers.

NOTES AND REFERENCES

1. Ainslie T. Embree, The Hindu Tradition: Readings in Oriental Thought, p. 229.
2. Kari H. Potter, Presuppositions of India's Philosophies, p. 259.
3. *Ibid.*
4. D. Chattopadhyaya, Indian Philosophy, p. 130.
5. Quoted in Eastern Mysticism, Ed. Raymond Van Over, p.4.

Bibliography

Abbott, Thomas, Fundamental Principles of Morals: Kant, Longman's London, 1909.

Aurobindo, Sri, Essays on the Gita, Arya Publishing House, Calcutta, 1950.

- -, The Riddle of the World, Arya Publishing House, Calcutta, 1941.

- -, The Life Divine, Arya Publishing House, Calcutta, 1947.

- -, The Problem of Rebirth, Sri Aurobindo Ashram, Pondicherry, 1948.

- -, The Ideal of Human Unity, Sri Aurobindo Ashram, Pondicherry, 1950.

- -, The Synthesis of Yoga, Sri Aurobindo Library, Madras, 1952.

- -, Sri Aurobindo Birth Centenary Library, Sri Aurobindo Ashram, Pondicherry, 1972.

Bishop, Donald H., Indian Thought, Wiley Eastern Pvt. Ltd., New Delhi, 1975.

Bowes, Pratima, Some Songs and Poems from Tagore, Allied Publishers Pvt. Ltd., New Delhi, 1984.

Brodov, V., Indian Philosophy in Modern Times, Progress Publishers, Moscow, 1984.

Chatterjee, Ramananda (Ed)., Golden Book of Tagore, Calcutta, 1931.

Chatterjee, S.C., The Nyaya Theory of Knowledge, University of Calcutta Press, Calcutta, 1950.

- -, An Introduction to Indian Philosophy, University of Calcutta Press, 1960.

Chattopadhyaya, Debiprasad, Indian Philosophy: A Popular Introduction, People's Publishing House, New Delhi, 1964.

Choudhary, Haridas, Integral Yoga, Institute of Asian Studies, California, 1970.

--, Sri Aurobindo: The Prophet of Life Divine, Sri Aurobindo Pathamandir, 1951.

Deussan, Paul, The System of the Vedanta, Tr. by Charles Johnston, Dover Publications, New York, 1973.

- -, The Philosophy of the Upanisads, Tr. by A.S. Geden, Dover Publications, New York, 1966.

Dasgupta, S.N., The Study of Patanjali, University of Calcutta Press, Calcutta, 1920.

- -, A History of Indian Philosophy, Cambridge University Press, 1955.

Davids, T.W. Rhys, Buddhist Sutras, (tr.), Dover Publications, New York, 1965.

Embree, Ainslie, The Hindu Tradition: Readings in Oriental Thought, Vintage Books, New York, 1972.

Gestering, Johnann, German Pessimism and Indian Philosophy, Ajanta Books International, Delhi, 1986.

Hiriyanna, M., The Essentials of Indian Philosophy, George Allen and Unwin, London, 1952.

--, Outlines of Indian Philosophy, George Allen and Unwin, London, 1952.

Jacobi, Hermann, The Jaina Sutras (tr: Sacred Books of the East), Oxford University Press, London, 1884.

Kulkarni B.K., Lokmanya Tilak's Metaphysic of Morals, University of Poona, Poona, 1973.

Lal, Basant Kumar, Contemporary Indian Philosophy, Motilal Banarsidas, Patna, 1978.

Landesman, Charles, Philosophy: An Introduction to Central Issues, Holt Rinehart and Winston, New York, 1974.

Mahadevan, T.M.P., Saroja, G.V., Contemporary Indian Philosophy, Sterling Publishers Pvt. Ltd., Delhi, 1983.

Maitra, S.K., An Introduction to the Philosophy of Sri Aurobindo, Banaras Hindu University Press, Banaras, 1945.

Maitra, S.K., The Meeting of East and West in Sri Aurobindo's Philosophy, Sri Aurobindo Ashram, Pondicherry, 1956.

Majumdar, A.K., The Samkhya Conception of Personality, Univ. of Calcutta Press, Calcutta,1930.

Mann, Thomas, Schopenhauer, Cassell and Co. Ltd., London, 1946.

Moore, Charles A., The Indian Mind (Ed.), Honolulu, Univ. of Hawaii Press, 1967.

Mill J.S., Utiliterianism, Everyman's Library, E.P. Dutton & Co., Inc., New York.

Muller, F. Max, The Upanisads, Dover Publications, New York, 1970.

- -, The Six Systems of Indian Philosophy, Longmans, Green & Co., London, 1928.

Nagaraja Rao, P., Introduction to Vedanta, Bhartiya Vidya Bhavan, Bombay, 1966.

Naletor, Igor, Alternatives to Pasitivism, Progress Publishers, Moscow, 1984.

Narvane, V.S., Modern Indian Thought, Asia Publishing House, Bombay, 1967.

Potter, Karl H., Presuppositions of India's Philosophies, Englewood Cliffs, N.J. Princeton Hall, 1963.

Prabhavananda, Swami and Manchester, Frederick, The Upanisads, Vedanta Press, Hollywood, 1947.

Puligandla, R., Fundamentals of Indian Philosophy, New York, Abingdon Press, Nashville, 1975.

Radhakrishnan, S. and Moore, Charles A., A Source Book in Indian Philosophy, Princeton Univ. Press, Princeton, 1967.

Radhakrishnan, S., East and West in Religion, George Allen & Unwin, London, 1949.

- -, Eastern Religion and Western Thought, Oxford Univ. Press, London, 1940.

- -, The Hindu View of Life, George Allen & Unwin, London, 1927.

- -, Indian Philosophy, George Allen & Unwin, London 1931.

- -, The Philosophy of Rabindranath Tagore, MacMillan and Co., London, 1918.

Rathakrishnan, S., The Philosophy of Upanisads, George Allen and Unwin Press, London, 1947.

Raju, P.T., Idealistic Thought of India, Harvard Univ. Press, 1953.

- -, The Philosophical Traditions of India, George Allen & Unwin, London, 1971.

Ramamurthi, Pratapgiri, The Problem of the Indian Polity, Longmans, Green and Co., Calcutta, 1935.

Rashadall H., The Theory and Food and Evil, Vol. II.

Sarma D.S., Essence of Hinduism, Bhartiya Vidya Bhavan, Bombay, 1971.

Sharma, Chandradhar, A Critical Survey of Indian Philosophy, Motilal Banarsidass, Delhi, 1964.

Singer, Milton, When a Great Tradition Modernizes, Preager Publishers, New York, 1972.

Sinha, J.N., Indian Realism, Kegan Paul Press, London, 1938.

Sources of Indian Tradition, compiled by Bary, Hay, Weiler & Yarrow, Motilal Banarsidass, Delhi, 1963.

Stcheribatsky, Buddhist Logic, Dover Publications, New York, 1963.

Tilak B.G., Gitarahasya, (tr.) by Sukthankar B.S., Tilak Bros., Poona, 1935.

Thibaut, Feorge, The Vedanta Sutra of Badarayana (tr.) Dover Publications, New York, 1970.

Underwood, A.C., Contemporary Thought of India, Williams and Norgate Ltd., 1930.

Vivekananda, The Complete Works, Mayavati Memorial Editions, Vols. I to VII, Advaita Ashram, Calcutta,1989.

Walker, Ralph C.S., Kant on Pure Reason (Ed.) Oxford University Press, 1982.

Yogendra Singh, Modernization of Indian Tradition, Thomson Press (India) Ltd., Delhi, 1973.

Zimmer, Heinrich, Philosophies of India (Ed.) by Joseph Compbell, Princeton University Press, Princeton, 1969.

Index